Praise for *Bobblehead Dad*

"'Funny,' 'witty,' and 'entertaining' are not words people typically use to describe a story about cancer. But Jim Higley's *Bobblehead Dad* isn't just about being sick. It's about the joy of living and discovering who you are, where you came from, and ultimately, where you want to be."

—TRACY BECKERMAN, syndicated humor columnist, "Lost in Suburbia," and author of *Rebel Without a Minivan*

"Jim Higley's soul-stirring memories of his Nebraska childhood strengthened him during his struggle with cancer. His life lessons are poignant, rich, and oh-so-genuine. The healing is real."

—SUZETTE MARTINEZ STANDRING, syndicated columnist and award-winning author of *The Art of Column Writing*

"The lessons that can be learned from Jim's courageous and beautiful story are invaluable. His touching words will evoke gratitude and push you to become a better person."

—MELINDA MARCHIANO, author and International Book Awards winner, *Grace: A Child's Intimate Journey Through Cancer and Recovery*

"Why wait for that 'smack on the head' to wake up and enjoy the precious moments of life? I highly recommend *Bobblehead Dad* to anyone who loves a page-turner! The pictures tell thousands more words!"

—**WADE ROUSE**, bestselling author of *At Least in the City Someone Would Hear Me Scream* and *It's All Relative*

"Jim is an insightful and passionate storyteller who has written the new 'must read.' In a unique 'bridging the time-space continuum' style, Jim's book is a reflection, an inspiration, and an entertaining and heartfelt read that is hard to put down. I heartily recommend it!"

—**SANDRA GEHRING**, Emmy Award–winning author of *Breaking Your Own News*

"Jim writes about how to find life in the nooks and crannies of everyday existence. He reminds us not to wait for an emergency to live—he reminds us not to wait for anything. Best of all, he shows us how."

—**JASON SEIDEN**, author of *Beyond Social*

"Jim Higley invites others to look more closely at the positive pivotal aspects of challenging life experiences by humorously and courageously sharing intimate insights from his own. Throughout this beautiful book, readers will discover the liberation and empowerment derived from uncovering the hidden gems in both the everyday and unexpected, leading them to their own journey of illumination."

—**ANNIE BURNSIDE**, author of *Soul to Soul Parenting*

"*Bobblehead Dad* isn't a story about cancer so much as it is the story of a man who faced cancer—and way too much of it for just one family. You'll fall in love with Jim Higley the child, and root for Jim Higley, the dad with cancer. *Bobblehead Dad* is a delightfully soothing read for any parent who has steered a family through difficult times."

—JEN SINGER, moderator, ParentingWithCancer.com, and author of *You're a Good Mom (and Your Kids Aren't So Bad Either)*

"As an empty-head dad, I highly recommend *Bobblehead Dad*. Jim Higley writes with warmth, humor, and optimism. He's also a great guy. Buy his book or I will come over to your house and drink all your beer."

—JERRY ZEZIMA, syndicated humor columnist for *The Stamford Advocate* and author of *Leave It to Boomer*

Bobblehead Dad

Bobblehead Dad

25 Life Lessons I Forgot I Knew

JIM HIGLEY

GREENLEAF
BOOK GROUP PRESS

Published by Greenleaf Book Group Press
Austin, Texas
www.gbgpress.com

362.196
H53B
2011

Copyright ©2011 James R. Higley

Distributed by Greenleaf Book Group LLC

For ordering information or special discounts for bulk purchases, please contact Greenleaf Book Group LLC at PO Box 91869, Austin, TX 78709, 512.891.6100.

Design and composition by Greenleaf Book Group LLC
Cover design by Greenleaf Book Group LLC

The term "Bobblehead Dad" is a trademark registered with the U.S. Patent & Trademark Office and is owned by the author.

Publisher's Cataloging-In-Publication Data
(Prepared by The Donohue Group, Inc.)
Higley, Jim (James Robert), 1960-
  Bobblehead dad : 25 life lessons I forgot I knew / Jim Higley.—1st ed.
    p. : ill. ; cm.
  ISBN: 978-1-60832-142-1
  1. Higley, Jim. 2. Cancer—Patients—United States—Biography. 3. Father and child.
4. Conduct of life. I. Title.
RC265.6.H54 A3 2011
362.19/6994/0092   2011923170

Part of the Tree Neutral® program, which offsets the number of trees consumed in the production and printing of this book by taking proactive steps, such as planting trees in direct proportion to the number of trees used: www.treeneutral.com

Printed in the United States of America on acid-free paper

TreeNeutral®

11 12 13 14 15 16   10 9 8 7 6 5 4 3 2 1

First Edition

For my three children—Kevin, Wallis, and Drew.
You teach me volumes. Every day.

Contents

Prologue

Long John Silver's seafood restaurant wouldn't have been my first choice as the backdrop for hearing what turned out to be the most powerful words my father ever shared with me. I guess things happen where they are meant to happen.

I was fifteen, and it was about a year after my mom had died. Eating Friday-night dinner at Long John Silver's—my dad's traditional way of observing Lent—became our weekly ritual after her death. It was during one of those visits, while my dad was enjoying his seafood combo and a cup of slaw, that I decided to throw a question out onto the table.

"So, um, do you ever sort of kind of think about wanting to do stuff, like—you know—like go out, um, on a date? I'm totally fine if you, you know . . . "

I'm not sure what possessed me to ask the question. Maybe I needed definition in the new world we lived in. I can't say for sure, and Dad never quite directly answered the question I had posed. But I knew I hit a nerve when—after a very long, uncomfortable pause—I received his direct, pointed, and purposeful response:

"I want you to listen carefully," he began. Were he a CIA operative, the tone of his voice would suggest to me that he was about to share the highest-level top secret information. But he wasn't CIA. This was my dad—breathing very deliberately and staring directly at me. I regretted asking the question as I sat there, still holding a fork to my lips.

He continued.

"I will raise you to be a man."

As I looked back into the depths of his eyes, I clearly knew they were telling me to utter not one more word.

And that was the end of our discussion. Never to be revisited again.

My dad fulfilled that commitment to me in the ensuing years. Spectacularly and selflessly.

It wasn't until after he died that I learned from his brother, my Uncle Jack, the reason for my dad's Long John Silver's message. When he was a teenager, my dad's mother died. And soon after, my dad's father remarried and began a new life with a new wife. My dad was told to find his own place to live.

Only then, after hearing Uncle Jack's words, did I understand the resolve I saw in my dad's eyes that night in Long John Silver's so long ago. I suspect that experience from his youth taught him the most important lesson in fatherhood he ever received.

Thirty years later, I myself was the dad. With three young children. And I was staring at a diagnosis of cancer. In retrospect, I was also about to begin the last chapter of my marriage—a painful period for my entire family which remains private. My world was collapsing on all fronts. For the first time ever, I feared for my own children's future as I came face-to-face with the realization that I may not live long enough to raise them to adulthood—let alone show them a father's unwaivering commitment.

Flying under the radar screen of life was no longer an option because I had plenty of things to address. Job one, however, was dealing with cancer. I not only wanted to win that battle; I needed to decimate the enemy—and reclaim the life I was meant to live.

And so began my journey toward clarity in becoming the man—and dad—I am today, raising my children with purpose and renewed commitment.

Hello. I'm a Bobblehead.

As a kid, I collected bobbleheads. As an adult, I had become one.

With four older brothers, I sort of inherited their old bobblehead dolls when I was a young boy. They were all baseball player bobbleheads. Truthfully, I didn't even like baseball that much, but I thought it was fun to play with the little figurines and their spring-loaded heads.

My favorite was a Mickey Mantle bobblehead. I liked seeing how long I could keep his noggin in motion with just the right flick from my index finger. Too hard and I'd end up with a spastic head jerk that came to a sudden stop. Too soft and the toy suffered the same fate. But when I found that perfect amount of pressure, I'd enjoy a bobble that would go on for a long, carefree bounce until the head ultimately rebalanced itself.

I was easily amused.

I also was fascinated by how Mickey's face would maintain a permanent, frozen smile no matter how fast or furious his head rocked.

Thirty-some years later, I was much like that bobblehead, going through the motions of life—perfect smile and all—just bouncing away. By all accounts, I was living a full and abundant life with my family and my career. And, to a great degree, I was. Maybe you knew me back then. I was firing on all cylinders, always in a constant state of motion, and looking pretty stable.

At the time, I even thought I was doing pretty well. But the truth is things were moving so fast in my world, I stopped connecting with the events, experiences, and people waiting for me in each day. I survived by bobbling.

My best bobbling, I'm ashamed to say, was saved for my three kids. Consumed with a job that had me leaving the house long before they were up, I was exhausted by the time I arrived home in the evening.

"Wudya do today?" was my standard question for the kids as I tried to connect in some way to the worlds that were theirs.

As a young grade-schooler, my daughter, Wallis, would always provide feature-length film descriptions of her day, recounting every eye-opening experience and emotion. Like helium escaping from a balloon, her words couldn't come fast enough. And there I was, wearing my Mickey Mantle smile, bobbling along and pretending to listen while many of her words ricocheted off me at lightning speed.

Bad. Bobbling. Dad.

Unfortunately, kids are smart, and they quickly sense when you're not really paying attention to them. So they stop talking and, eventually, just grunt or nod.

That's how we became a bobblehead dad and his three nodding children.

When I reached the age of forty-four, however, my bobbling came to a screeching halt. It was much like the day—as a child—I accidentally stretched Mickey Mantle's head a little too far and snapped the spring. When my own bobbling world snapped, I found myself with an entire summer at home removed from all of life's obligations.

How does a middle-aged guy manage to land an entire summer off? Well, I had cancer. It's something my parents and siblings encounter with regularity. Some families have red hair. Or they spawn a lot of tall people. Mine produces very ordinary people who have a propensity for cancer. So I had plenty of training under my belt when my own world was turned upside down with surgery and a summer at home to heal.

But this is not only a cancer story. It's a story about a dad who had a chance—at the halftime show of his life—to stop bobbling and relearn many of the life lessons he'd forgotten. It's a story that reveals the meaning found in simple moments and the people who fill them.

Most importantly for me, it's the story that unfolded a road map to living the second half of my life with intent.

Note from the Author

To help you rediscover some of your own life lessons, reflective questions are provided for each chapter on page 185.

Chapter 1

Some Things You Don't Want to Inherit

I SPENT A fair amount of time as a child playing in a closet. This was by choice, mind you, and I actually enjoyed it. The closet was on the second floor of our home, located in a small town and surrounded by nothing but Nebraska cornfields. Tucked up under the roofline, this little room had a slanted ceiling and no windows. I pretended it was my tree house. I'm not sure of its exact size, but it was plenty big enough for me to lie down and stretch out my scrawny body in any direction I chose.

We referred to it as the "game closet" because on the left side was a wall of shelves filled with an assortment of games and puzzles that

---

Above: Tom is between my parents. Dave is in front of my dad. Mom has Mick's neck in her gentle grip. That's Kevin in the plaid shirt with me in the front.

rivaled the children's aisle in our local drugstore. I'd spend hours at a time in that closet pulling out game after game onto the prickly, green carpeting. I'd set up Mousetrap just to watch the cage wobble down the plastic, notched pole and trap the mouse. I'd pull out Life and spin the wheel countless times to see how many turns it took to get my car all the way around the board. I'd play one-man Twister. I'd want desperately to attempt Operation, but ours never seemed to work. And I wouldn't even bother with Risk. It seemed too complicated.

You'd think that with four older brothers I'd have had plenty of people with whom to play games. But it didn't work that way in our family.

My oldest brothers, Tom and Dave, were twins and nearly nine years older than me. Mick and Kevin were also older—four and five years, respectively—and inseparable from each other.

Then there was me, the odd man out. The fifth player in a world of games meant for four. The little brother on the sideline while everyone else played two-on-two.

Thank goodness for my mother. She was happy to let me hang out with her. And I was usually content to be with her. It didn't matter what she was doing—cooking, laundry, cleaning, gardening, grocery shopping, or running errands. She was good company. She liked to talk. She liked to give me jobs. And she knew how to keep me busy.

My mom was always around. Her job was to run the house while my dad was at work every day. I didn't know too much about her own childhood other than something bad had happened when she was twelve, and her father left forever. I also knew that her mother died of cancer when I was just a baby.

We usually could find our mom maneuvering around our undersized kitchen to whip up her round-the-clock buffet line or in the basement surrounded by volcanic piles of dirty clothes. She never got sick, but she went to appointments regularly with an old man named Dr. Hill who helped her with what she referred to as "a little blood pressure problem." She treated herself to a weekly visit to the beauty parlor. She rarely drank, but her eyes would light up when someone offered her an occasional strawberry daiquiri.

Her world was her sons. She was the lioness, and we were her cubs. And while she was quick to put each of us in our place when needed, God help the foolish soul who ever crossed or criticized any of her offspring.

She didn't mince her words. She said what was on her mind. She was very clear. And she could brilliantly give a verbal tongue-lashing while still leaving the recipient feeling as though he or she had just been handed a plate of homemade cookies.

Ask our pastor and the entire parish council, for instance. I believe her fundamental issue with them—back in the early seventies—was how parish funds were being allocated within our parish school. My mom, as well as many others, felt the athletic program—which I should point out involved all of her children—received a disproportionate amount of funds at the expense of music, theater, and arts—which involved none of her children.

It infuriated her; so much so that she did what no one else would do. She took on years of favoritism, documenting her thoughts in a three-page, single-spaced letter that became the talk of the congregation. The parish council, all men, had no idea what hit them.

All I know is not long thereafter the band was enjoying new uniforms as well as a newfound celebrity status thanks to their new cheerleader, my mom.

By the time I entered ninth grade, all of my brothers were out of the house, and I was starting to savor some independence from my parents. That was my perspective. Perhaps my parents viewed it as living with a snotty teenager. Either way, I had the entire second floor of our house to myself. I had access to all the clothes and electronics my brothers had left behind. I was making new friends. All in all, life was pretty good.

That all changed one spring day during that same school year.

A couple of buddies were over one night visiting me because I had just been released from the hospital after an appendectomy a few days earlier. That same night my mom became violently sick. It was her head. Headaches. Bad stuff. An ambulance came.

The next eight days were somewhat of a blur as my brothers, Dad, and I kept vigil in a fluorescently lit hospital waiting room. They believed it was a stroke—bleeding in the brain. She was in a coma for most of that time. Of course, we thought she'd get better. She was strong. She was our mom. Bulletproof.

She died on March 18.

A few weeks later, I came home from school one day and found my dad sitting in the family room crying. He was holding a letter from my mom's doctor.

"It was cancer," he said. "Mom had brain cancer." He said it over and over. "Inoperable." "Incurable." He also told me something I had never heard before: she had long feared that she would die of cancer.

It was at that moment I inherited her fear.

I STARTED PLAYING a game shortly after my mom died, and I played it brilliantly for years. It's actually a game a lot of people turn to after tragedy knocks on their door. I call it the *Immunity Game*. A therapist might call it denial. It's a game where you convince yourself—because you've gone through something really bad in your life—that you're immune to other pain, sadness, or loss for a long, long time. It's basically a free pass you give yourself.

An effective game, it helped me move rather smoothly through my teen years, my twenties, and well into my thirties.

But even with the crutch of the *Immunity Game*, I still lived with the same gnawing fear my mom had known for her forty-nine years on this earth. Like an eyelash that grows backward and constantly pecks at your eyeball. It was there. Cancer.

Funnily enough, I didn't even understand what cancer *was* for a long time. It was just the enemy. If I had a headache, it was brain cancer. Sore groin? Testicular, no doubt. I self-diagnosed that three times. And every time I got a clean bill of health, I'd think to myself, *Of course! No bad stuff for me! I've got immunity!*

And that would hold me over until the next apparent medical crisis.

Unfortunately, regardless of how diligently I played the *Immunity Game,* it didn't work for me. Or any other Higley. Our family was an easy target.

Gold medal losers.

My dad died of ureteral cancer when I was thirty-six. I celebrated my fortieth birthday with my dying brother, Kevin, who was suffering from the same brain cancer my mom fell victim to twenty-five years earlier. Before I reached the age of forty-one, our family scorecard was not good at all: Mom, Dad, and Kevin had all lost their lives to cancer. Only three of my brothers and I were left.

Each successive loss made me come to terms with the reality that no *Immunity Game* was being played. Cancer is a fierce and unpredictable competitor.

There were likely more battles ahead.

Lesson 1

The scariest

bogeyman

is the one

in your head.

JUN · 92

Chapter 2

Why Painters Use Drop Cloths

IT WAS MARCH. Winter was ever so slowly giving up its hold on long, cold days—providing an occasional surprise with a warmer, sun-filled afternoon.

Our living room was getting a facelift—new furniture and curtains—and Granny Smith green had been chosen as the new, delicious color scheme. The last remaining thing to be done was paint the room.

Now, painting a room is not a monumental task. In fact, I have always taken pride in being rather handy with a paintbrush—as evidenced by my having single-handedly painted every square inch of the inside of our first two homes in Durham, North Carolina.

Above: My brother Kevin holding my son Kevin.

Actually, several rooms in those two houses were painted *twice*; it seems I had a knack for painting a room and then deciding it looked *nothing* like what I had anticipated based on the tiny color chip I had originally picked out at the paint store. I ultimately learned the value of investing in a quart of paint of the proposed color, trying it out on a small section of wall, and then—and only then—moving ahead with my final purchase of several gallons of paint.

But for some reason, painting the living room green in our new home in Chicago had become a burden for me. I didn't know if it was the kids' busy schedules, my work, or my age. Perhaps it was just the annual slump I go through every March as I privately relive the memories of my mom's death, which return predictably every year like Chicago's weather patterns. Whatever the reason, I had lost the energy to tackle a weekend painting project.

However, this one particular weekend in March was different. Something was changing in my life. I could feel it in subtle ways. And I actually felt excited to take on the living room.

Painting day was set for Saturday. And as luck would have it, my son Kevin and my daughter, Wallis, were invited to attend a show in downtown Chicago that day.

That left my youngest, Drew, a six-year-old at the time, home with me.

No problem, I told myself as I developed strategies for keeping Drew busy all day with a refrigerator full of treats and an armful of videos.

With everyone else out of the house, and Drew happy as a clam in the basement, I was ready to get to work.

My first step whenever I paint is always to lay down drop cloths. I like big, serious drop cloths, not the wimpy, thin, plastic type that comes folded up in little packages. I buy industrial-strength 100-foot rolls of clear plastic. The thicker the plastic, the better. It's easy to roll out. It cuts great with a sharp knife. And it doesn't slide around when you walk on it. It's serious protection and I always feel safer knowing it's there.

Choosing *where* to start painting is the most important decision for me. Do I start on a wall that's easy to finish—providing some quick gratification? Or do I start on a more complicated wall—leaving the easier ones for last?

For this particular project, I decided to start on the wall with the big bay window—which provides my favorite view from the inside of our house. This wall had a fair amount of trim work, but it also had good lighting. *An acceptable compromise*, I thought.

Drop cloth down.

Ladder set.

Paint stirred.

My work began.

I follow a process when I paint. I tackle one wall at a time. I use a two-inch angled brush to do the wall's edging first and then I use a roller, filling in the large open areas. I continue this process in a clockwise manner around the room (never counterclockwise!), completing one coat of paint on each wall. If needed, I go around the room for a second lap, applying another coat of paint.

Not more than five minutes into painting the first wall, standing on the ladder with the top of my head grazing the ceiling, I realized something. I was happy. It was a feeling I hadn't felt in many months.

Nine months to be exact.

My brother Kevin had died nine months earlier and I missed everything about him. In addition to missing him, I also knew I missed the life I had when he was still a part of it. It had been a lonely nine months.

As I worked my way along the underside of the crown molding, my mind shifted to memories of doing "handyman" projects with Kevin—painting, wallpapering, carpentry, laying tile. Kevin and I were the guys in our family who could work with our hands. We were good partners.

Kevin was a photographer. He spent most of his career working for the Gannett Newspaper chain, and the Associated Press and national magazines regularly picked up his work. He spent a career covering politicians, entertainers, sports figures, and other celebrities. My family watched the Super Bowl religiously every year—but not to enjoy the game. We were far more interested in looking for Kevin on the sidelines with his telescopic lenses and wearing his bright yellow "PRESS" vest.

Kevin was thoughtful. Kind. He always took care of the underdog. Quietly, and without any fanfare. I remember him rallying some of the other photographers to reroof their secretary's house one weekend. Why?

"She's a nice lady. She needs help," he told me.

Compassion came instinctively for him.

My mom loved to tell the story about a sweet five-year-old Kevin sneaking into my nursery in the middle of the night to give me a bottle. And it was Kevin who rushed me to the hospital when I nearly sliced off the tip of my left index finger with a razor blade when I was eleven. It's a wonder we weren't super-close as kids. But then again, he had five years on me.

We became close, though. Somewhere along life's path—through grouting, wallpapering, and trips to the local hardware store—we became extremely close.

And for the first time since he had died, I was starting to feel alive. I had known for a long time that I needed to move forward and come to terms with Kevin's death. But knowing something and feeling something are two different things.

It was in that moment, however, that I could actually feel Kevin's presence. I felt his warmth and his calmness.

I was embraced by a feeling of safety and security I had never before felt in my life.

Footsteps. A startling sensation made me aware of the sound of footsteps from my vantage point on top of the ladder. Then, I heard muffled noises and chatter from Drew, who was directly below me in the basement. At first I thought it was the movie he was watching. But then it was eerily quiet and soon Drew ran up the stairs to the first floor and into the living room.

"Hey there, Drew. How's it going?"

"Good."

"Stay off the drop cloth. I spilled some paint over there."

"Daddy?"

"What's up, Bud?"

"I have a question."

"Fire away."

Drew didn't really need to share his question. I knew what he was going to ask. It was as if I were watching a movie I had already seen before.

"Daddy, are angels real?"

"Sure they are, Drew."

"OK."

"Why do you ask?"

"There's an angel in the house."

"No kidding, that's neat. How do you know that?"

"I was talking to him."

"That's cool, Drew. Anyone we know?"

"Yeah. It's Uncle Kevin. He's here right now. I was just talking to him in the basement, and he told me he isn't sick anymore."

My heart was pounding through my T-shirt. Kevin *was* here. As I looked down at Drew from my perch on the ladder, I realized—in that brief moment—I had never felt so peaceful and content.

But as good as that felt, I wasn't really sure what it meant.

I'M GOOD ABOUT getting an annual physical.

Hypochondriacally good.

Right after the first of each year, my inner clock reminds me to schedule it, which usually places me in the doctor's office sometime in February. My "forty-three-year-old" physical was originally scheduled for mid-February, but due to a work conflict it had to be canceled. I let months go by without rescheduling it, but I kept a Post-it note with the words "reschedule physical" stuck to my desk. Finally, a couple of months after my forty-fourth birthday, I scheduled my physical for October.

I had just about reached the point where I was going to skip that appointment, though, and restart the annual physical thing the following February. After all, I had followed the rules of the *Immunity Game*, which meant I was safe for years, right? My dad and my brother had died in the previous few years, so I probably had at least ten years of protection. Immunity is such an awesome feeling. In the end, however, I went.

The October physical was uneventful. Blood pressure—*check*. Eyes—*check*. Ears—*check*. Throat—*check*. Heart, lungs, abdomen—*check, check, check*. I stopped by to see the nurse, Jean, before I left, to provide a vial or two of blood and some other routine samples—all per the orders on the paperwork from my doctor. With that done I was on my way, thinking to myself I was good until the following year.

The following afternoon I was at an off-site business meeting with Tom, a guy who worked with me. We were holed up in some conference room trying to focus on a new initiative when my cell phone rang. It was my doctor's office calling, and I debated whether or not I should take it. Normally I would have let it go to voice mail, but my instinct said otherwise. So I stepped out into the hall.

Surprisingly, it was the doctor himself, tracking me down to go over my blood test results.

"Everything looks fine, generally speaking."

After hearing those opening words, I started to tune out and refocus on what Tom and I had been discussing. But the good doctor continued.

"Blah, blah, blood sugar, *blah,* little high, *blah, blah,* LDL, *blah . . ."*

When I thought he was winding up, I remember starting to tell him I'd look forward to seeing him the next year. But then he threw in the unexpected comment that there was *something* he wanted to ask me.

"Sure, what is it?"

"Did you ask me to run a PSA test?"

PSA. PSA. Think. Think. *Blood test,* I thought. Older guys. Prostate. *Yeah, prostate, that's it.*

"Um, no, I didn't ask for anything. Why?"

"That's odd. I don't request a PSA test until a man is fifty—and I know I wouldn't have marked it down for you to have one unless we talked about a family history. But we got your PSA number and it's a little high. Do you have a history of prostate cancer in your family?"

"No. I have lots of cancer in my family, but no prostate cancer."

"Well, I'm sure it's nothing. Probably a lab error. Maybe I just accidentally checked the 'PSA' box on your paperwork. Tell you what. I'll sleep better if you have this checked out by a specialist who can run a more sensitive test than I can. I have a name and telephone number for you. Promise me you'll follow up with this other doctor?"

He didn't need my promise. I placed that call and set up an appointment with the specialist before I stepped back in to pick up where Tom and I had left off.

Somewhere in those few brief moments, while Tom was mapping out our rollout schedule for our initiative, I started my journey to an unknown place.

After I sat down, I wondered if Tom would be able to read my face. I was feeling a smorgasbord of emotions. Fidgety. Anxious. Confused.

But the one thing I didn't feel was fear. I had felt fear before and knew what it was like. I sat there while Tom continued to speak words I didn't hear, taking a mental diagnostic check of my inner workings.

Fear was registering at a zero.

What was registering off the charts, however, was the same feeling I had had a couple years earlier when I was on the ladder dipping the brush into the Granny Smith green paint. I felt safe. And secure.

What I felt was my brother Kevin. I knew he had something to do with that PSA box getting checked off.

And I had every reason to believe he'd stick around to make sure I had plenty of drop cloths under me.

Lesson 2

Loved ones

die, but

they

never leave.

NOV · 78

Chapter 3

Playing Post Office

I NEVER UNDERSTOOD exactly what my dad did for a living. He ran something we referred to as "the plant." What I did know was that the plant was an odd configuration of large warehouse-type buildings on the edge of town. The farthest buildings held expansive storage racks with different types and sizes of lumber. In the remaining buildings a group of men worked five days a week—from 7:15 in the morning until 3:15 in the afternoon—building a variety of wooden store fixtures that were used to display merchandise for retailers. The biggest one was named Montgomery Ward. I had a pretty good understanding of what the "men" did at the plant. But I never fully grasped my dad's role.

Above: At Dad's office. A few years after my lessons on how to sort mail.

He wore a suit to work, which differentiated him from everyone else. I knew he was important because he not only had an office, he had an office with gold letters on his door that spelled out his name: Robert L. Higley. He also had a lock on his door, a clear signal to me he was a man with clout. Beyond that, my dad's business world was a dark hole.

I did know one thing about my dad's job, however. I knew what he did at the plant every Saturday morning.

He sorted mail.

I knew this because I was allowed to witness this task weekly.

My Saturday journey to my dad's office was always the same. It was the only time of the week I was allowed to sit in the front seat of his car. There were very few words spoken between us because my dad was more focused on the radio—listening to the melodic words of someone named Paul Harvey. That always seemed to put him in a good mood. Halfway to the plant, we'd stop at the local post office, where my dad would leave me in the running car while he ran into the simple, brick, one-story building. I was never allowed into the post office. My job was to wait patiently for three or four minutes until my dad reemerged with his mail.

The stack of envelopes my dad carried under his arm each week was always bundled together with very large rubber bands and was usually about six or seven inches thick. After placing the bundle between us on the bench seat, my dad would put the car into "drive" and ask me if I was ready to go to work.

I was always ready to go to work with my dad!

Getting from the post office to the plant was only about a two-minute drive, but for me it was the longest two minutes ever because I spent all of it trying to assess the possibilities that might await us in each Saturday morning's mail. Most of the envelopes looked routine— and likely held the usual letters and other boring stuff. Sometimes, however, there were packages that clearly contained something far more interesting, such as a calendar or a pen with the name of his company printed impressively on the side: Watson Industries. Those were the packages I wanted to get my hands on!

We always parked in the exact same space—the one closest to the front door. I always carried the mail from the car into my dad's office. My dad always hung his coat and my coat on the two hooks behind his door. I always sat in my dad's one wooden guest chair while he, of course, sat in the leather chair with wheels.

Sorting mail was a ritual for my dad. My job was to learn from the master.

With the rubber-banded pile placed before him on his desk, the lesson would begin.

Step one was opening. In this step, my dad swiftly cut open each piece of mail. He started with the top envelope, opened it, and turned it upside-down onto a new pile. This task was completed—without words—with each successive envelope. At the end of this step, there was a new pile of "opened" envelopes, all turned upside-down.

In step two the master would take the entire pile of envelopes, flip them back to the original order, and set them on the desk. He was now prepared to remove the contents of each envelope in the same order he had opened them. As best as I could tell, this step was more art than science because I could never quite figure out a pattern to his actions.

The specifics of this step included (1) extraction of the contents of each envelope; (2) a brief scan of the contents (sometimes requiring a quick "flip-over" to look at the back side); (3) discarding of the envelope (or sometimes stapling it to the papers inside); and (4) placing the contents of the envelope into one of several new piles being created in the middle of the desk. In the end, there were four new piles; the one on the far right was held together with a large paperclip.

The four piles quickly turned into three as the contents of the far left pile were swiftly discarded into a green metal garbage can located on the floor next to the desk.

The following step involved the pile that was next to the discarded pile. This pile also had a very short life; my dad picked it up, walked to the rear of his office to a wall of multicolored metal file cabinets, and—within minutes—filed all of the contents of the pile into various drawers.

Two piles remained on the desk.

Then came the moment—as it did every week—when my dad would open the thin center drawer of his desk and pull out a dime from a plastic box.

After placing the dime on the pile clasped by the large paper clip, he'd slide the stack over to me. The master was almost done with the day's work—at least the part I was allowed to witness.

"I'll see you in a little bit," he'd say with a wink.

That was my cue to take the clipped pile and carry it to Mr. Johnson's office and put it in a blue tray that had two big letters—"AP"—on it. After that, I was free to take the dime to the lunchroom and treat myself to a soda pop.

Then, I waited. Wondering what the master was doing with that last remaining pile.

———

YOU'D THINK IT would be simple to get an official cancer diagnosis if, in fact, you had the big "C." It wasn't simple for me, however. It was a six-month journey during which blood tests "looked suspicious" and biopsy after biopsy revealed nothing. Details of a prostate biopsy aren't something you want to hear about, so let's just say it feels like you have electrical probes shoved up your bottom hatch only to be followed by a doctor setting off a colossal Fourth of July fireworks show in there. I have never sweated—or shed tears of pain—so much.

The first three biopsies didn't find any cancer cells. By the time they did the fourth biopsy, I honestly just wanted some resolution.

Good or bad. Unfortunately, I got my wish one Sunday afternoon when my doctor called me out of the blue to go over my results.

When I heard his voice, I knew what the news would be.

He gave me a bunch of medical information. Numbers. Doctor talk. I had him repeat everything a couple of times so I could write it down. In an instant, a disease I had been reading a fair amount about suddenly moved from the remote "third person" perspective to the intimate "first person" one. And I was that person.

He told me to call his office the following morning to set up an appointment for Tuesday so we could discuss our action plan in person.

"Try to enjoy the rest of your weekend," he said before we hung up. What else could he say?

I couldn't move after finishing that call. Moving meant leaving the past behind. Moving meant facing the reality of the future. But standing still—frozen in the moment with the phone still in my hand—also made me aware of how alone I felt at that moment. *Who do I turn to?* I thought. The only people at home were Kevin and Drew, fifteen- and nine-years-old at the time. Wallis, thirteen-years-old, was on her way home from a volleyball tournament in Minnesota.

Months and months of emotions began to percolate up from my secret hiding place deep inside. I feared I was about to explode emotionally—something I didn't want my two boys to witness—so I got myself outside, to the porch on the back of our home. It was an insignificant place I had walked through hundreds of times en route to someplace else. But that day it became the venue for the meltdown of my life. Curled up on the floor, with my knees pulled up to my face, I pressed up against the railing and sobbed.

I found myself wondering how my dad and brother reacted when they found out they had cancer. I was sure they didn't end up on the back porch in a fetal position wailing like me. They were strong. And as much as I wanted to be strong, right then I also just wanted to cry. I wanted them to call out to me and tell me what to do.

"Dad!" I heard faintly through the back door. It was my son Kevin shouting for me.

I didn't want to be busted on the porch so I cracked open the door and yelled back into the house, "I'm outside. I'm on the telephone!"

"Baseball, Dad! We have to go!"

I had forgotten that Kevin and Drew had their weekly batting practice at an indoor baseball clinic about thirty minutes away. And we were going to be late.

Batting practice, as it turned out, was a good distraction for me. Sitting and watching them play ball gave me the time I needed to sort things out in my head. It was my first experience in living my life with cancer. I was surprised at how settling it felt simply to be there.

I decided I couldn't panic. I needed to tell people in a thoughtful manner. I needed to get organized for my doctor's visit in a couple of days. And I needed to try to reclaim a little bit of normalcy by making dinner for my family.

I'm not a cook, but that night I cooked. I pulled out a dusty recipe book and followed directions to the letter for making lemon chicken and rice. During dinner, I learned all about Wallis's tournament in Minnesota. I learned that Drew hates capers. And I learned that Kevin suddenly looked more like a young man than a little boy. In retrospect, it was during our lemon chicken dinner—with my secret still safe—that I finally allowed the spring under my bobbling head to snap.

Unable to bobble, I could now relearn to live.

Later that night, I went up to Kevin's room to tell him about my doctor's call. Kevin was always a mature kid, and I know what I had to say added ten years to his 120-pound frame.

Unfortunately, it was Wallis who I caught off guard. I took her into the living room, the Granny Smith green living room, and sat her on the couch. I ignorantly wasn't prepared for her reaction. In retrospect, I see that she was a child who had lost her grandfather and uncle to cancer in the previous few years and now, here was her dad, dropping another bomb in her life. She came undone. And the only thing I knew to do was to hold her in my arms, allowing her to cry until there were no more tears.

My emotional well was empty. It was late. Talking to Drew would have to wait until the next day.

After everyone was asleep, when I finally crawled into bed, I not only wanted to turn off the lights in my room; I wanted to turn off the nightmare I had just walked my family into.

My alarm went off Monday morning at 5:00 AM—as usual. What was not usual was that I just stayed in bed, flat on my back, for about fifteen minutes after I shut off my beeping wrist alarm. I remember thinking one thing: my life would never be the same again. It was the first day I woke up with cancer. At least officially.

I hated that thought.

That morning, I did something I hadn't done in a long time. I lingered around the house for a couple of hours enjoying the morning routine of my family. There was absolutely nothing eventful that morning—although the big kids, Kevin and Wallis, looked at me differently. Tentatively. Drew was still the only one who was able to go through his morning motions unscathed. But there came a time when I had to take some of his innocence away to let him know Daddy needed an operation.

By eight o'clock, I was at Caribou Coffee, ready and equipped to spend the entire day. I had brought along all of the articles on prostate cancer I had been collecting over the last few months. I had two books on prostate cancer I hadn't yet looked at. I had a dozen new folder files. I had my cell phone and laptop. I had a couple of highlighters, some pens, and a desire to be productive.

The first thing I had to do was sort through everything. One by one, I scanned every article, trying to ascertain whether or not it was applicable to me at the time.

I made three piles. One was to throw away. The second consisted ·

of articles I thought might be important in the future. The last pile was the one I wanted to focus on and understand that day.

Around ten o'clock, I had finished my sorting project. The "throw away" pile—which was the largest of the three—was gone. Banished. Not important anymore. The articles in the "hold-onto-but-file-for-later" pile were now separated into about half a dozen file folders, each appropriately labeled with a title, such as "Diet Information," "Clinical Trials," and "Support Groups." They might be of interest to me someday—but not today.

Today's business was to get my arms around things so I could have a productive meeting the following day with my doctor. Distractions weren't on the agenda.

I needed to be prepared.

I also needed to give things away. For me, that meant my business obligations in the coming days. With a few phone calls, my work distractions were gone, handed over to trusted colleagues who—not to my surprise—eagerly jumped into my life and took responsibility for handling my workload for as long as necessary.

I felt organized. Now I was ready for the primary task of focusing only on what was important. And I still had more than twenty-four hours before I was scheduled to see my doctor. Things were coming together.

With a fresh cup of coffee in front of me, I pulled out a pen, a highlighter, a notepad, and my two books. I knew I would never be able to read each book in full. So I did the best I could. I started with the more technical one. Chapter by chapter I worked my way through it. Some parts I read in detail; some parts I scanned. I took notes and wrote questions down as needed. As I moved through the book, I was actually amazed at how much I already knew. What had felt overwhelming to me just twenty-four hours prior was, page by page, becoming something that was understandable which made the cancer a little less threatening. It was like confiscating the opposing team's playbook ahead of time. Knowledge is a good—and comforting—thing.

By mid-afternoon I had finished book one, *Surviving Prostate Cancer*, and had amassed a dozen or so pages of handwritten notes and questions. With the heavy reading behind me, I moved on to the next book, titled *Prostate Cancer for Dummies*. I kid you not. It was actually a terrific check against the first book, which read more like a medical textbook. Five o'clock that evening was quitting time, and I was ready to put my research down and go home.

That evening, I gave myself the gift of watching television with the kids.

My meeting the next day with my doctor lasted a couple of hours. We sat in his office and talked about a variety of options. Unfortunately, almost all of his "options" weren't for me. For me he reserved the granddaddy treatment—a radical prostatectomy. He then proceeded to show me diagrams of the surgical procedure, detailing step-by-step how he was going to slice my belly open and skydive in for the kill. I felt like I was being sold a set of Ginsu knives as he shared his assortment of propaganda and pamphlets

"I've done this hundreds of times," he said, trying to reassure me.

What I wanted to ask him was, when he said "hundreds" did he mean 102 or 998? As if that even mattered. He knew I was on board and he knew I trusted him. With or without the complimentary steak knives. Surgery was scheduled for the following month.

As we were wrapping up, my doctor said he tells his patients that getting to the point we had reached in our consultation is much like putting a whole bunch of information through a funnel. With cancer, there are so many issues to work through, but the objective is simply to sift it through the funnel and to focus on the important things that emerge.

Interesting, I thought to myself.

He sees it as a funnel.

I see it as sorting mail.

Lesson 3

Clean

your desk.

Clear

the clutter.

Then focus.

JAN · 75

TUNNEL
TO THE RIVER

Chapter 4

I'm Sorry, What Did You Say?

THE SUN WASN'T shining when my mom died, so it must have been nighttime. My brothers and I were together in the hospital waiting room when my dad told us she was gone. We were never a family of huggers. But we learned how to hug that night. That was also the first time I saw my father cry. He was speechless—and could only focus on the logistics of getting his five boys home safely.

I ended up alone in the car my dad drove back to our house. A traffic jam of questions was lodged in my throat, honking to escape. But nothing came out. I just sat in the silence of the front seat watching headlights passing on the left side.

Above: A great winter trip to California—and Disneyland—with my folks. My mom died two months later.

Once home, I escaped to my bedroom, behind a closed door. I knew the lights would never go off that night and resigned myself to spending the next several hours under the protective shield of over-sized headphones listening to an Olivia Newton-John album over and over again.

The next morning our house was stuffed with people. Everywhere. My mom's kitchen was taken over by her closest friends, who were scurrying around opening cupboards and laying out trays of food, which made our kitchen look like the backdrop for a bake sale. Random people were using the kitchen phone. My mom's phone. She loved it because it was red. She doodled on the pad of paper next to it. But people weren't doodling on it that day.

The entire scene wasn't right. In fact, it was hauntingly wrong. And I couldn't stay there.

I found refuge on our front porch. I was hoping one of my friends might show up and rescue me from the happenings inside our house. That friend never came. But the high school's biology teacher did. "Coach A," as all the kids called him, had coached my brother Mick a few years earlier in both track and cross country. He only knew me as the little brother standing with my dad. But he and Mick were close, so I wasn't surprised to see him show up at our house that morning.

I looked up at Coach A as he walked up to the porch.

"Mick's inside," I said, looking back down at my shoes.

But Coach A didn't go inside. Instead, he sat down next to me on the front steps. He said nothing. He just patiently gazed straight ahead with me, looking past our front yard and into the emptiness beyond.

"Your mom taught you a lot," he eventually said, penetrating our silent dialogue. "Ya gotta keep those lessons alive." I nodded.

"Don't ever forget that, OK?" he ended.

I nodded again. I heard what he was saying, but I had no clue what he meant. My mom was just my mom. What was I supposed to keep alive?

AS WORD OF my diagnosis spread through the various circles in my life, I had countless conversations with friends, relatives, and coworkers. These were caring conversations. Reassuring conversations. Conversations focused on this general belief that everything would be OK. It seemed, somehow, that everyone had magical powers with which to see into the future. And what they saw was always good.

"I know you'll be fine," they repeated constantly.

While I appreciated the sentiment and optimism, I found that comment funny. In many ways, I felt as if people were trying to gain *my* reassurance, which I found hard to give convincingly.

I'm candid. I'm blunt. And while I certainly wanted to have a positive attitude, I was also realistic. I knew this story could play out in many ways. After all, our family batting average was terrible.

Two of the conversations during those early days, however, were truly stop-you-dead-in-your-tracks-and-shake-you-by-your-shirt-collar moments.

The first, and most powerful one, was with a casual friend named Karen. I had known her tangentially for several years because she was a friend of some of my good friends. But our paths rarely crossed. She was about my age. Petite. A glowing, energetic person. I knew she had had her own issues with cancer a few years earlier, but that was the extent of what I knew. She was simply Karen—my friend's, fun, spirited friend who had had breast cancer. Little did I know she would become one of the most influential people in the story of my life.

Her first contact with me arrived as a voice mail. "Jim, it's Karen, Sarah's friend. I'm so sorry to hear what you're going through. Listen, I know you're buried, but I really want to talk to you. I have something to tell you. It's important. Could you call me when you have a few minutes? Thanks!" Click.

I was intrigued. I was curious. And I wanted to meet Karen immediately. So we did. The very next day.

Karen's talk was the most motivating, uplifting conversation ever. Not just during that period in my life. I mean ever. We didn't talk about her own experiences through surgeries and recovery. We didn't talk about the beating her body had to endure through her treatment. We didn't talk about being afraid. Karen had only one thing to teach me.

"Jim, you are going to receive the most amazing gift as you go through this," she promised.

I took mental notes as she shared with me the extraordinary gift she ultimately received as the result of her journey.

It was like a moment from the *Kung Fu* television series I used to watch as a child. There was always a scene when the little boy would sit in front of old Master Po, who would say, "When you can take the pebble from my hand, it will be time for you to leave."

I wanted the pebble Karen was holding.

"You may not even realize it at the time, Jim," she said, "but if your mind and heart are open, I promise you will come out of this with a gift that will change your life.

Your gift will be yours and yours alone. And you will never be the same. Regardless of what happens with your cancer."

She also gave me a notebook.

"Write, Jim," she said. "Take time to write."

For the first time in days I was excited. Karen framed my life in a way no one else could. Not only was I filled with her energy but I was also beginning to experience a new taste of my own.

Karen came to teach me a lesson. And I listened.

There was a gift out there with my name on it.

Lesson 4

Welcome good advice with action.

Chapter 5

Give and Take

IT'S INTERESTING TO me that my mom, who had the most wonderful gift of gab, was given few opportunities to speak during the final eight days of her life. Perhaps that is what makes her last words so poignant.

My mom was moved to a hospital in Omaha the day after she was taken away from our house in an ambulance the night of March 10, 1975. Having her in Omaha, which was about thirty miles away, gave us hope.

It gave us hope that some magical team of doctors who we had never met before would take care of her, fix whatever was wrong, and send us all back to the world we used to live in.

Above: Mom enjoying a very rare, quiet moment in the kitchen.

My four brothers, Dad, and I spent the last eight days of my mother's life in a dimly lit, brown-toned waiting area off a wide, sterile hallway in the intensive care unit. While I don't know much about camping, I think there must be some sort of similarity in the bonding that takes place among total strangers in a hospital waiting room—especially in the ICU—and a campsite. My family had a particular corner of the waiting room we took over day after day. Other families followed the same routine, each staking out their own area. As new families joined us, we all embraced them with a compassionate understanding of what they were going through. Most families stayed a day or two and then disappeared from our lives because their loved one had improved. Some families, however, were more like ours; their story was complicated. I learned over time that when one of those families moved to a special inner waiting room—basically a smaller room off of the large waiting room—their loved one was close to death.

It was a room I never wanted to be sent to.

During those eight days, our routine was identical. We were allowed to be with my mom—usually two of us at a time—for ten minutes every hour. My dad would decide which of my brothers would join him for each of those visits. I refer to them as "visits," but actually they were nothing close to that. My mom slipped into a semi-coma early on so our time with her was spent holding her hand, stroking her arm, or brushing her hair while we talked about who had visited that day, what the weather was like, or how beautiful the newest bouquet of flowers was. How much she was aware of I will never know. What I do know, however, is that it was the only time I can recall my mom relinquishing her nurturing role in our family. For once, we were taking care of her.

At times she would open her eyes and stare into the void of her room. A few other times she actually "woke up" and was able to speak a word or two, share a grin, or pucker her lips to blow us a kiss. But those moments were rare.

One of those moments, however, was with and for me.

I was in my mom's room with my dad. She had not been alert for over a day. For about fifteen seconds, though, she forced opened her eyes and shared with me the last words I ever heard her speak.

"I'm sorry," she said as I gripped her hand tighter.

"I'm sorry I can't take care of you anymore."

For me, that was the end.

Within a few days, our family found that our time had come to be in the small, inner room off the main waiting room.

We stayed there until she died.

With her death, while Dad took over the dual parenting roles, my brothers and I tried to pitch in and fill the many voids left by our mother.

I assumed several of the "around-the-house mom" jobs in our family even though I was only fourteen. I was probably the one best trained—at the time—to tackle some of those jobs because I knew so many of the tiny details my mom had quietly taken care of for all of us.

So, while my dad dealt with all of the heavy lifting that came with the loss of a parent, I was able to provide some of the small continuity in our family, our home, and our world that made the absence of our mom a little less painful.

I was good at cleaning. Or organizing a closet. I rallied everyone to decorate the house at Christmas. I took care of some of the random things my mom was in charge of like planting the gardens. I was good at keeping tabs on everyone and felt the responsibility for fixing things when there were problems.

I became a caregiver. And I remained one ad infinitum.

WHILE KAREN'S PROMISE of an awaiting gift put me in the right frame of mind for my entire cancer journey, it was my close friend Chris who helped put something else into perspective in what turned out to be the second most meaningful conversation I had shortly after learning I had cancer.

"Listen to me, Jim," he said to me over the telephone after I called him to tell him what was going on. "This is your turn to let other people take care of you. And I think you'll stink at doing that. You've got to let us—the people who love you—give something back to you."

I couldn't find the words to reply. At first I felt as though Chris was stripping me of my role in life.

"Chris," I said after a long pause, "I . . . I don't . . . I don't know."

I knew how much Chris cared for me. But I could tell from the tone of his voice that he wanted to make sure I was listening to him. He was offering me something very tangible, but I wasn't quite getting it.

"Then you just defined my job, Jim. I'll make sure you find out what it's like to be taken care of. I'm going to ride you and make sure you experience what it's like to be taken care of."

His words were finally sinking in. I felt as though Chris had somehow flipped on an old movie reel that started playing scenes from my life in my head. With each passing scene, I began to understand the recurring role I played in so many relationships.

For the more than thirty years since my mom had died, I was a "go-to" guy. I was the fixer. The rock. I could steady any ship.

The problem with being that guy is you eventually believe you really *are* as strong as you try to appear. Then you begin to thrive on being viewed as that person. But the reality is everyone has limits—and I had long surpassed mine.

So I learned to bobble to compensate. It was the only way I knew how to keep the illusion in motion.

I have known Chris for twenty-plus years. We met as young men, fresh out of college, living in Chicago. He was a squeaky clean stockbroker and I had just started my job with a real estate development firm. We were introduced by a mutual friend and eventually started hanging out together through a volunteer group we both became involved with. Our friendship was solidified the day we met. Chris and I are very similar. Frightfully similar. He's the first person I would call in a crisis. And he's the only person I would call to share my excitement about a new way to better organize and store Christmas decorations.

Need I say more?

Chris is also a caregiver. A doer. An organizer. A solver. A fixer. A believer. And he's one of the few people who could tell me point-blank what was in my best interest and have the impact he did.

He was right. It was time for me to take a break from the bobbling. I had some healing to do.

Chris was inviting me to a place I hadn't been to in a long time. I was not only ready to go back.

I needed to.

Lesson 5

The best

caregivers

have received

the best care.

Chapter 6

I Can't Believe You Said That

IT WAS A couple of weeks after my mom died. I was fourteen and just beginning to grasp the reality of what had happened. I was feeling something I hadn't yet felt since the beginning of the ordeal surrounding her death a few weeks earlier. It was a void bigger and deeper than anything I had ever experienced. And although as a fourteen-year-old I still thought I knew everything, I was only starting to understand that this new life—the one without my mom—was actually going to last forever. I found myself desperately trying to catalog every possible memory of her. Would I remember her smile? What did her eyes look like? Would her voice actually slip away too?

Above: I'm at the top. Then Mick, Kevin, Tom, and Dave.

I wanted someone to come along and fix everything. I'd have negotiations with God where I'd promise to do anything—anything at all—if he'd give me my mom back. I'd create scenarios in my head where she would walk through the door, alive and well, and tell us the story of how she had been part of a top-secret government project that required her to fake her death for national defense purposes.

I wanted her back. I didn't care how. I didn't care about logistics. I just wanted her back.

One day, a family friend stopped by our house shortly after I got home from school. I was getting used to people visiting. Usually they were dropping off food or a batch of cookies. I also knew they were checking in on me. Conversations with these people were always the same. They'd tell me what a wonderful mother I had. They'd tell me a favorite story about her. And most times, they would cry. This particular friend, however, had a message that had yet to hit my ears.

"You know," she said, "you're really lucky because your father is still young enough to remarry. And you can kind of have a new mom."

Yup. I guess my whole perspective was just plain *wrong*. Lucky me. Lucky Dad. This could all be resolved by introducing a new woman into our lives. Let's start taking applications!

Hearing this family friend's bizarre words was the first time in my life I realized the absurd, insensitive things people sometimes say at the wrong time. It was my initiation into the world of hurtful comments people throw out when, oddly enough, they think they are being helpful.

OUCH!

My dad, who had been battling cancer off-and-on for a few years, was finally losing the battle. He had been hospitalized and was close to death. Ever since the day my mom had died, I dreaded the day I would lose my dad. Intellectually, I knew it was bound to happen. But

I always hoped that day would be far into the future.

He was seventy-two, and the future was now.

He had lived a fabulous life. He was given not only one but two wonderful marriages. We were all blessed when he found love again in the one woman, Arlis, who had the strength, compassion, and inner confidence to join our testosterone-filled family. My brothers and I knew we had so much to be thankful for as we each spent time with Dad in the hospital during those last couple of weeks of his life.

We had been down this path before, with our mom—twenty-two years and nine months earlier. Hospital waiting room moments with my brothers—for both my mom and my dad—are probably some of the most intimate, personal ones I've ever shared with my siblings. All of life's distractions are gone. The focus is so simple. It's all about coming to terms—individually and collectively—with the looming departure of both a person and a part of your own life.

A day or two before my dad died, I was in the waiting room alone with my brother Kevin. We were talking about our dad, about the life he gave us, about how lucky we were, when a family friend entered the room and stumbled into our conversation.

"How's your dad, boys?"

"Well, he's still telling jokes, so he's good."

"Have you decided what you're going to do about his funeral and where he's going to be buried?"

Kevin and I were speechless. Dumbfounded. Blown away. Did this guy actually just ask such an insensitive question? He came all the way out to the hospital to ask us where our dad—who was still very much alive—was going to be buried?

DOUBLE OUCH!

My brother Kevin's life ended at the age of forty-six. Brain cancer. Just like my mom. He fought for eighteen months—during which time he gave every member of our family the most amazing collection of memories and love.

Kevin did not have any children, yet there was no one in our family who connected with kids as well as he did. No one remotely close. Everything about Kevin was cool, especially through the eyes of a young person. He brought such joy to each of my three children, especially my oldest child, who is named after him.

When Kevin died, we all died a little. Actually, we all died a lot. Kevin was so much a part of our family and his death extinguished a spirit within each of us.

"Thank goodness he didn't have any children."

I heard that comment regularly after he died, as friends tried to support and comfort me. I don't mean merely a couple of times, either. Over and over, people would offer their condolences to me with some commentary about how lucky we all were that Kevin didn't have any kids.

Clearly, I understood they were focusing on a concept that no children would have to endure the loss of a parent. I, more than most people, could empathize because I *was* one of those children many years ago. What people didn't understand was that, with Kevin's death, our entire family was mourning the loss of one thing—Kevin.

We didn't feel fortunate about anything. There wasn't a bright side to this story.

TRIPLE OUCH!

I SUPPOSE I should have expected it. I suppose my prior experiences should have prepared me for what I was about to encounter as soon as they gave me the official cancer diagnosis.

"Thank goodness it's only prostate cancer. You'll be fine!"

"My seventy-five-year-old uncle was diagnosed a few years ago with the same thing and he is doing great!"

I was overwhelmed with how many times I heard comments like that. Daily.

I wanted so desperately to jump back with an answer, to let people know their comments weren't making me feel any better. I wished they could hear what my doctor told me so they might begin to understand this wasn't a little issue.

"A young guy like you shouldn't have this kind of cancer," my doctor said. "Something's very wrong when a guy your age deals with this."

To put it into perspective, roughly 200,000 men in our country are diagnosed with prostate cancer each year. And with less than 1 percent of those men in my age bracket, I was in a club with very few members.

So, while I needed many things, sugarcoated comments weren't high on that list.

I needed reassuring words, most definitely. But I didn't expect anyone to say things to make it all go away. Life can be hard. I get it.

Some things can't be fixed instantly—if ever.

I really just needed to hear people say, "I care."

Better yet, I needed someone to say, "I will be there for you. You won't be alone."

And if they weren't comfortable with words, I would have simply loved to get a great big hug.

Lesson 6

When you
can't be brilliant
with words,
be brilliant
with your arms.

FEB · 65

Chapter 7

Mom and Dad Were Doing It

IT WAS A Saturday afternoon shortly after the first of the year. I was four, and my brothers and I were home watching ABC's *Wide World of Sports* on television—a weekly ritual that took place in our family room. Typically our dad was right there with the five of us while our mom could usually be found a few steps away working in the kitchen. This particular week, however, they were somewhere else in the house doing "parent" things—presumably for a long time—which was apparent because our mom had made an extra large bowl of popcorn for us to share while we watched one of only four channels available to us on our black-and-white RCA television.

Above: That's my dad on the right. Just in case you couldn't tell my parents apart!

I actually learned a fair amount about sports watching that television show with my brothers. Living in Nebraska, we had absolutely no exposure to professional sports. The closest thing we had was the University of Nebraska's football team, which was more of a religion than a sport to us Cornhuskers. Through television, however, it didn't matter that we lived in a small town in the middle of cornfields. With the flick of a switch, we were in Yankee Stadium or watching downhill skiing in Austria. Places we could only dream about going to.

What I learned that day, however, had nothing to do with sports. I learned something about my parents. I learned what they did in their bedroom when the door was closed.

My brothers and I had been watching the program for thirty or forty minutes—long enough for my mind to wander. I was a curious kid, even a little nosey at times. I liked to know everything everyone was doing. And with four brothers, a mother, and a father, I had plenty to keep tabs on. So, while my brothers yelled at the refs and the players—watching that week's "thrill of victory and agony of defeat"—I set out to find my parents.

They were in their bedroom with their door closed—an odd circumstance for a Saturday afternoon. I heard whispering. Then laughing—actually more of a stifled giggling noise. I couldn't imagine what was happening on the other side of the door. What I did know was it sounded fun and I wanted to be a part of it! Inquisitive preschooler that I was, I had no choice. I opened the door. And I will never forget what I saw.

My parents were wearing tutus!

Both of them. Tutus—as in ballerina outfits. My dad had on a pink one, and my mom had one that was an aqua color.

I stood there staring at them, with one hand still on the door handle, as they both stared back at me in dead silence. All three of us had our mouths hanging down to the floor. I knew I was in so much trouble.

Then, I saw my parents look at each other and spontaneously

combust into laughter. Theirs were the kind of grown-up laughs I'd heard on *I Love Lucy* reruns on television.

My mom's eyes were brimming with tears. She fell on the bed holding her stomach as she laughed harder and harder, fanning herself with her hand. My dad had to lean over, with his hands on his knees, as he tried to get words out in between his hyena sounds.

"Costumes, Jimmy," my mom said between her laughs. "We're going to a party wearing costumes."

I had no idea what she was talking about. I was just loving the show.

Over the years, I began to realize how important laughter was to my parents' relationship. It was one of the cornerstones of their marriage because they not only knew how to laugh, they knew when they needed to laugh.

Most importantly, they knew that laughter was often the best medicine for tough times.

CANCER ISN'T FUNNY.

And I wasn't doing any laughing the first few days after I received my confirming biopsy results.

Sunday was the surprise call from my doctor.

Monday was the day of research.

Tuesday was meeting with the doctor to finalize plans.

Wednesday was sharing the news with friends.

By Wednesday night, after the word got out, I had nearly thirty messages on my answering machine at home.

Each message was a carbon copy of the previous one. *"Jim, I just heard what's going on. I am so sorry. But I know you'll be fine. You're strong. I know you're buried right now, but call me when you can. And let me know if there is anything I can do for you."*

Finally, I found something that made me laugh.

These were messages oozing with love. I knew and appreciated that. I just found the quantity of calls funny. Crazy. Unexpected. Who gets thirty messages? Was I really going to call people back? And what was I supposed to tell people to do? There were probably so many things I did or would need, but I didn't have a clue at that moment. What I did have was the return of my warped sense of humor.

I've got an idea, I thought to myself. *Maybe I could tell all these people there is something they can do! I'll tell them I'm* registered! *Brides do it. Even grooms do it. Why can't a sick person?!*

The absurdity of my idea made me laugh out loud. It was as if the release valve on a pressure cooker was finally opening up, and a bunch of steam was spewing out into the air.

I could only imagine the confusion on people's faces if they actually heard this silliness. Most would know I was teasing, of course. But I'm sure a few people would be stumped—especially if I did a new greeting on my answering machine:

"Hi, you've reached the Higley house. We're swamped with all this cancer crap. For those of you wondering what you can do, I'm now registered at Crate and Barrel, Eddie Bauer, and the local hardware store. Thanks for your concern!"

So maybe that was good for a quick chuckle and a little escape. But the truth was, I was scared. 24/7 seriousness is draining. It feels like a constant beating with a stick.

Initially, the idea of laughing was hard to even imagine. I'd see funny things on television or in the newspaper and know I should laugh, but I couldn't. It's really hard to laugh at the outside world when your own world is crumbling.

But when you are raised with the gift of laughter, as I was, it can't stay suppressed forever. It's too powerful. Thank goodness for that. I eventually could see bits of ha-ha in my own life. Certainly not in the cancer, but in the mind-blowing circumstances that suddenly consumed my life. And laughing at parts of those experiences made me feel a little more alive.

The funniest part of it all was that the more I allowed myself to laugh, the more therapeutic my tears became.

Both ends of the spectrum of emotions had meaning.

Lesson 7

Meaningful

tears

fall from eyes

that know

how to laugh.

Chapter 8

Growing into My Running Shoes

I WAS NOT a very good athlete as a little kid. At least that's what my four older brothers frequently told me. They had me convinced the Higley "athletic gene pool" had a supply big enough for just four boys. Being boy number five, I lost out. And I never really had enough faith in myself to try to prove them wrong. So I went through grade school petrified to play sports.

But in sixth grade I decided to join the track team. Or maybe my parents forced me—I can't remember. What I do remember vividly, though, was my mother handing me a pair of Mick's old running shoes that were held together with duct tape. Other than that, all I got was a

Above: I not only wasn't a runner. I wasn't a basketball player, either. That's Dave (far right) and Mick (center), each holding a basketball. I think I'm holding a bag of cookies.

big hug and her reassurance (I wasn't convinced) I'd have fun.

"How hard could it be?" I tried to tell myself. Three of my brothers—Tom, Dave, and Mick—were runners. They each ran cross-country. They each ran track. And, lest anyone fail to remind me, they all were good.

Maybe I could be good too, I hoped.

So I signed up. Hesitantly.

During the first week of practice, the coach assessed everyone's skill levels. I have no doubt he assumed I came to the team as a mini version of my older brothers.

"Little Higs, I wanna clock you in the 440," he yelled.

I stunk at that.

"Let's try the 100," he screamed.

Nope again.

"Maybe distance." I'm sure he was praying as he stood on the side of the track.

Another dismal effort on my part. The coach must have speculated I was adopted. As for me, after this series of trials? I wanted to run—in the opposite direction.

While I suspect the track coach thought long and hard about making me the team manager—or worse yet, the guy in charge of the water cooler—he ultimately had me run hurdles: 100-yard low hurdles. Everyone, including me, understood his strategy. At that age, a couple of kids never even made it to the finish line in the hurdles because they fell down. If I could simply clear the wooden hurdles I'd at least have a chance of not coming in last place.

It was a sad way to compete, but it occasionally worked. And I found myself savoring—a few brief times—some of the athletic prowess I felt had been reserved only for my brothers.

I don't remember ever quitting the team. But then again, I don't remember finishing the season, either. I was one of those guys who drifted away. I'd make up an excuse to miss a practice. Then one or two more, which eventually kept me from participating in the few track meets on the schedule. So I just stopped going. And no one ever asked me to come back.

I hated sixth-grade track. But more than anything, I hated walking away knowing my brothers were right.

I wasn't a runner.

IT WAS NEW YEAR'S DAY. My cancer diagnosis wouldn't arrive until a few months later. Our family had gathered around the kitchen table to enjoy a traditional southern meal—something we picked up from our thirteen years in North Carolina—including hoppin' john, black-eyed peas, and collards. It was a meal meant to bring "good luck" and, for us, a meal of good memories.

I had decided that January 1 would be the perfect opportunity to share some very big news with everyone: I was signing up for a triathlon in July.

Considering I hadn't run more than a mile in well over ten years, I thought this was big news. I had been mulling over the idea in my head for months after watching the Chicago Marathon the prior fall. Seeing so many people run that day, including many who were physically challenged, inspired me and made me believe in my abilities. I was tired of seeing myself as the little brother who couldn't do things. And I knew announcing my intentions to my family would get me off and running.

My announcement brought only one reaction: stares from my kids. Stares that pretty much said, "*You've-got-to-be-kidding-us-dad-like-you're-totally-the-last-person-we-can-imagine-competing-in-a-triathlon.*"

I guess they actually were listening to me all those years when I proclaimed myself the non-athlete in the family.

"Come on guys, give me a break! I'm going to be forty-five in August. This is something I really want to do."

Not less than two minutes post-announcement and I was already starting to doubt myself. But I was not going to back down. So I pulled out a triathlon book I had secretly been reading over the prior few weeks to show everyone the training schedule I was about to kick off. Maybe that would get them excited.

Unfortunately, they had more interest in clearing the dirty dishes.

So my big news on New Year's Day didn't create the memory for which I had hoped. Yes, I was a little ticked. A little hurt. But, regardless, I was now officially preparing for a triathlon.

Over the next few months I trained hard. I swam twice a week. I ran three times a week. I lifted weights. I followed my regimen to the letter.

More than anything, though, I was having fun and feeling confident. I was enjoying the daily experience of what I was doing. I was relishing little things like short runs in my neighborhood with my young son, Drew, riding his bicycle alongside me. Life was good. Everything was good.

Everything, that is, except the stupid thing my doctor detected during my annual physical. Somehow, one simple blood test morphed into several months of other tests. I suddenly found myself chasing my triathlon dream while my doctor was chasing the possibility of cancer hiding somewhere in my body. It was hard to keep those two races separated.

I tried to hold together my training in March and April, but I was also undergoing more and more tests—which meant more and more doctors.

Eventually, my training started to slip. Not terribly, but it did slip. I never once imagined, however, I wouldn't do the triathlon. It was only April, and I still had three months ahead of me to get ready.

But everything changed on that Sunday when my doctor called me with the news they had found the cancer. Even while he was talking about surgery, I was thinking it would happen three to six months down the road. So when he said something that included the words "surgery within six weeks," I had the wind knocked out of me.

After I hung up the phone from that conversation, when I was alone crying on our back porch, my mind was racing through millions of feelings. One of the things I kept obsessing on was all of my triathlon training. I felt silly to have made it such an important part of my life. I was questioning why I had spent so much time in the prior few months getting ready for something that was not going to happen.

The next several days following that Sunday were like a bad dream. What was originally scheduled to be a Tuesday lunchtime swim was replaced with a meeting with my doctor to discuss surgery, risks, and recovery. My early morning weight training time was spent reading, researching, and note taking on every possible issue I could get my arms around. And the evening runs with Drew at my side became my time to call family and friends to bring them up to speed on my "news."

Those first few days were exhausting. But by the end of the week, most of the big decisions had been made, and the explosive craziness born the prior Sunday was starting to be replaced with focus and resolve.

Ironically I had long scheduled a getaway trip with old friends from North Carolina for the end of that first week. I was confused as to whether or not we should all still go on the trip, but eventually I made the decision to go, convincing myself a break would be good. We all arrived in Santa Fe late Thursday afternoon and were so happy to see each other. It felt safe to be with trusted friends. Although we had much to catch up on that first night together, we were all tired from the travel. So, after a quick stroll around the hotel and an abbreviated dinner, we all turned in for the night.

I was tired but not quite ready to sleep. It had been an emotional, challenging, cancerous week. I started a fire (with a flick of a switch!) in the adobe fireplace. Pulling up a chair to absorb the heat, I sat and thought.

Hypnotized by the flames dancing behind and between the fake logs, I let my mind re-create the realities of the last several days. My body felt peaceful and relaxed. But I also found myself questioning everything. Maybe I wasn't really relaxed? Maybe I was avoiding reality? My thoughts danced around until I finally told myself I had to flip the switch inside my head for the night. It was time for me to go to bed.

My body has an internal clock, and it is set to wake me up at 5:00 AM every morning. And unless I am extremely tired, my clock works well. It was working the following morning. But with the different time zone, it meant I was up at 4:00 AM Santa Fe time. And when I wake up, I'm up.

It was still pitch-black outside. I could see the moon through the window. I grabbed a blanket and went back to my chair in front of the fireplace, which was still burning. I found myself picking up my thoughts from the night before. Random thoughts. What was I feeling? What was I supposed to feel? I wasn't afraid. Should I be?

Eventually, the sun began to appear. It was going to be a beautiful day. I knew no one else would be awake for at least a couple of hours. And as happy as I was sitting in front of the fireplace, I knew I needed to move.

I needed to run.

And even though I didn't feel the pressure of training for the triathlon, a run sounded right. It sounded perfect. So I changed, strapped an iPod to my arm, and slipped outside.

Drops of mist were still hanging in the air. I walked about a block or so, stopping occasionally to stretch and dial the iPod to a new Rascal Flatts album my son Kevin wanted me to listen to. By the time the second song began, I picked up my pace.

I started up Canyon Road, the fifty-yard line for most of the art galleries in Santa Fe. We had walked part of it the prior day, marveling at many of the seventy-some galleries that lined it on either side. The road had a slight incline. Something I hadn't noticed the day before.

I also hadn't noticed the beautiful pots of flowers that were periodically set out in front of several of the galleries. There were wooden fences with peeling paint next to rusty, wrought iron gates. But they all breathed newness in the morning light. I was fascinated by the homes behind the galleries and didn't think twice about looking through the windows to catch a glimpse of the lives inside.

I wondered how some of the galleries got their names.

A white dog with brown and black spots playfully ran with me.

On the side of the street, I saw a child's red tricycle with a bent rear wheel and I smiled. *Someone forgot to bring in his toy last night!*

Before long, I found myself at a "T" in the road. Which way? Left looked good. And left turned out to be great.

I wound myself along the Santa Fe River. It's called a river, but it's more of a creek—a beautiful one at that. I was curious how cold the water was. I wondered if it all ran into a lake. There were sporadic clusters of rocks that broke the water and created a wonderful ripple effect in the current.

Other runners started to appear. All smiling and raising a hand to say "good morning!"

I took a street to my right. It looked residential and appealed to my sense of morning adventure. Newspapers were still lying in the driveways. Nice homes. People must enjoy living there. What kind of jobs did they have?

I liked the album I was listening to—*Feels Like Today* by Rascal Flatts. I was glad Kevin downloaded it for me. Suddenly, the lyrics of one song, "When The Sand Runs Out," started to register with me . . . la, la, blah, la . . . "an old friend's grave."

I felt my heart pounding faster through the sweat-soaked shirt stuck to my chest. I slowed down just enough to rewind the song and listen to it again. It was about a man who died after living a life that wasn't complete. He didn't take chances. He didn't experience the richness of life.

I felt as if a spotlight had suddenly been shone upon me. And I was sure that everyone—even though there was no one—was aware of me as I stopped to rewind the song and listen to it as I let the resonating final words sink in.

"Yeah, I wanna be runnin' when the sand runs out."

I had 17 million goose bumps prickling my skin. My earlobes were dripping like a leaky bathroom sink. My eyes burned with salt. My shoes and socks were soaked. And I had never felt more alive than I did at that moment.

I wondered if this was the gift Karen had promised me I would discover. Ever since I had spoken with her, I was on the lookout for something big. It was a positive distraction if nothing else. But it also caused me to analyze everything in my life because I truly wanted to find "it." I wanted validation.

But at that moment of revelation, I simply let my steps become purposeful.

A detour through the residential streets eventually led me to market square in the middle of town. Craftsmen were starting to display their art on rainbow-colored blankets under an arcaded walkway. My pace slowed down to an easy walk as the soundtrack in my ears came to an end. I uncorked the earphones from my ears so I could hear the sounds of the morning unfiltered. I stopped to admire everything. The delicate silver rings one artist was proudly arranging looked like soldiers lining up for the morning's drill. An older, smiling woman displayed her brilliant beadwork. I knew my daughter, Wallis, would love it all. I made sure I looked at the vendors' faces. I wanted to see their eyes. I wanted them to see me smile at them.

As I strolled back to the hotel, I came upon an old Catholic church. There was a familiarity to it. Paradoxically, the cold, austere stone exterior seemed to extend an embrace to me, so I approached it and found an open door.

Inside, there was a small chapel where a mass was being celebrated in Spanish. I stood there, seeing only the backs of the faceless parishoners, and listened for a few minutes. Incense floated in the air.

I walked to the main sanctuary and found a place to rest in an empty pew. I closed my eyes. With the distant murmuring of the Spanish liturgy in the background, I explored the catacombs of my life. I thought about the amazing twists I had experienced. I thought about my mom. My dad. My brother Kevin.

I thought about my children and the dad they needed me to be.

With statues of saints looking down on me, I kept going back to that call from my doctor the prior Sunday. I remembered sobbing to a depth I never had before. I marveled at all I had learned in the few days since. At the top of the list was a realization of how much I still had to learn. Life was throwing me curveballs, and I was confused about so many things. But in spite of all that, I felt empowered in a new way because I realized, finally, this about myself.

I *was* a runner.

Lesson 8

There's only one

person stopping you

from being who

YOU

were meant to be.

Chapter 9

Mum's the Word

MY MOM'S IDEA of a garden was limited to a couple of terra cotta pots with orange marigolds set out on the front porch each summer.

With five boys and a yard that usually looked more like a school playground, her minimal gardening efforts probably made a lot of sense. Boys and gardens don't mix. Throughout the course of a typical summer day, our yard would be home to baseball games, Frisbee throwing, makeshift driving ranges, go-cart riding, and squirt gun fights—including not only the five Higley boys but also a broad mix of neighborhood kids.

Above: That's me standing in front of Mom's mums. Season two!

So, my mom was wise not to let any gardening interests compete with an army of boys and the arsenal of balls and toys that came with them.

That changed, however, one fateful September Saturday.

My mom had gone to visit an elderly lady from our church, leaving the five of us at home to enjoy a modified version of two-on-two basketball. (That meant my four older brothers were playing against each other while I ran around the court pretending to contribute to the game.)

After a couple of hours, we started wondering when our mom would be home. It wasn't that we really missed her, mind you. The real reason was she had promised to make her weekly quadruple batch of chocolate chip cookies for us upon her return. When my mom baked cookies, she did so at "army-levels"—which meant plenty of bowls and spoons for all five of us to lick. Thus, by the time she pulled into the driveway in her wood-paneled, light-blue Ford station wagon, we were already savoring the thought of her creamy cookie dough.

"I have a surprise!" she blurted out.

Surprises from my mom almost always meant food. But she had already committed to baking cookies before she left, so this one stumped us. Had she gone to the grocery store and bought us each a package of our favorite type of cookie? That was a ploy she would use sometimes when she didn't have the time or energy to bake.

"We give. What's the surprise?"

"Follow me," she said as she walked to the back of the car and opened the rear door.

We all peered in and saw her surprise.

Three or four short brown boxes, each holding what looked to be plants. But they weren't in pots. They were, well, kind of dug up, with clumps of dirt around the roots.

That was the surprise? Our mom brought home boxes of green weeds?

"They're mums!" exclaimed our way-too-excited mom. "My friend dug up some of her yellow mums, and she said this is a perfect time of year to plant them!

"Here's what we're going to do," she started to explain. "I think we'll pull up the grass in the area between the sidewalk and the house. We'll plant the mums there—in front of the bushes. And then, early next summer, we'll plant some other bright flower in among the mums. We'll have fun—and it's going to be beautiful!"

She was on a roll. She had a vision. A mission.

And she kept using the word "we."

"Should *we* get started?"

My mom rarely asked for help. And when she did, she got it. No questions. Within minutes we were all in front of our house, taking directions from her. We had become garden boys.

The area she chose was a semicircular space—about twenty feet long and six feet wide. It was the space between the curvy front sidewalk and our house. Since the day my parents had built the house six years earlier, this area always had grass—with a few bushes up against the house.

My older brothers' job was to remove the grass. It was fascinating for me to see how they could take a shovel and peel the grass back, revealing the roots lying underneath the surface. We tossed all of the pieces of grass into a few fifty-gallon cardboard barrels my dad brought out from the garage. And in about fifteen minutes, what once had been a grassy patch was nothing but dark, smooth Nebraska dirt.

Next my mom carefully laid out the contents of her boxes—thinking through the spacing of the dozen or so plants. I refer to them as "plants," but by this time they were mostly limp and looking more like candidates for the fifty-gallon cardboard barrels. But my mom saw past all of that. And after she planted and watered the last of her new treasures, she stood back, smiled, and said, "Next year, this will look great!"

If only she knew.

The following spring, after a long, cold, snowy winter, the mums started to show signs of life. A little worse for the wear, they obediently sprouted an abundance of new leaves and buds on a daily basis.

As planned, during the Memorial Day weekend my mom planted the balance of the flowers in her garden. White alyssum—a low ground cover—lined the front while red geraniums found their home in front of the yellow mums. It all looked a little sparse. But my mom didn't mind.

She loved her garden. She'd water it. She'd weed it. The garden was on the south side of our house, so it soaked in the sun. It was also next to our driveway, however, and unfortunately received its share of out-of-bounds basketballs.

But the garden—especially the mums—flourished. My mom was right. It did turn into a thing of beauty. And Mom soon became known as the lady with the big yellow mums.

The second year, her mums continued their exponential growth.

And by the third season, the mums were about as big as the bushes behind them. My mom's enthusiasm, on the other hand, was getting tempered. The mums were not only huge; they were woody and taking on a life of their own. And while she tried her best to trim them back, they only seemed to come back stronger and bigger each year.

They had become the primary resident in what had become her garden from hell.

Until, that is, my mom was talking to a friend about her out-of-control situation and learned a secret.

"We need to split our mums!" she announced.

Splitting mums—thinning them out—was a fundamental practice learned in Gardening 101. The only problem was my mom had never taken that course. She never knew.

Out came the shovel.

Swoooooosh!

A vision of a guillotine went through my head as I watched my mom work her way down the row of mums, digging part of them out, thinning them away from the plants that remained.

She had been given the key to unlock the mystery of a happy garden—and gardener. And it worked.

From that day forward, the front garden once again became something my mom enjoyed. It was no longer overwhelming to her. She was in the driver's seat.

Because she knew when to split her mums.

FASCINATING. IT WAS absolutely fascinating to me how every outside obligation in my life seemed to disappear as fast as I could say, "Hey, everybody! I have cancer!"

I've always been a doer. A leader. Like most forty-something-year-olds, I juggled a full plate of work, family, and volunteer activities.

In a warped way, however, I started believing that having little time for a good night's sleep meant my days were busting at the seams with extremely important things. Bobblers think that way.

Bobblers also think novel-length "To Do" lists are really impressive.

I wasn't always like that. But somewhere in the last twenty years, weekends became nothing more than the two days after my Monday through Friday work routine during which I could tackle my lists. Most regrettably, somewhere in those twenty years, my self-worth became partially tied to how many tasks I could complete, begin, push, juggle, organize, or document.

After my cancer diagnosis, I rarely said to anyone I needed to back off. I rarely sought permission for relief from duties and responsibilities. People simply took those loads off of my shoulders. Friends, associates, acquaintances—and in some cases, virtual strangers— made all of my responsibilities go away upon hearing what I was dealing with.

It was exhilarating.

People from work sat down with me to reallocate the minutia of my business obligations. Folks in the volunteer groups I was involved with surprised me by "volunteering" to assume some of my duties. My friends stepped in. So did my family.

Nowhere was this more evident than with all the ridiculous things around the house that were under my domain. Faced with the reality of a couple of months of being laid up, I had to teach someone how to do the long laundry list of stuff I was the resident expert on. That someone was my son Kevin.

A couple of weeks before my surgery, I started to spend time with him each day teaching him one thing at a time. Like how I had the shelves in the basement neatly organized with lightbulbs based on their wattage. Or where my special sawed-off broom handle was so I could masterfully get a broken garbage disposal to start again. I taught him where the alarm was for the septic system. I showed him the meticulous details of the electrical panel in the basement. I taught him the daily and weekly requirements of our pool, including how to clean out skimmers, how to add water, and how to perfectly place the chlorine tablets into the dispenser.

It was, in reality, a lesson in Dad's insanely organized and ordered world. Kevin was too kind, too sweet, and too loving to ever tell me what I'm sure he was thinking.

"Dad, I've got it covered. And, by the way, you're nuts. None of this is complicated. I'll be fine!" He didn't have to ever say that. I was thinking it to myself.

For a guy who thrives on order, this was a revealing process as I was forced to dismantle the puzzle of my life, piece by piece, and give things away. The truth was the more pieces I gave away, the more I understood that much of "my stuff" was trivial at best. It was humbling, for sure, to face the reality that many of the things I filled my life with weren't all that important. But they seemed to be.

And the longer I did them, the more important they became. Just like my mom's mums.

Growing out of control.

Lesson 9

Unless you have
a gardener,
you're in charge
of splitting
your own mums.

Chapter 10

The Real Dirt

THE GARDEN WITH the yellow mums was just the beginning. During the next few years, our yard was transformed into a mini-botanical garden.

My mom's second garden was more a product of necessity. It was a couple years after she planted her mums, and my parents had recently built an addition onto the back of our house, expanding what was a way-too-small family room. The project also included the construction of a new patio, directly behind our garage.

When construction was near completion, the area adjacent to the new patio was a war zone. The grass was a disaster, filled with tire ruts, construction debris, and an assortment of trash.

Above: My parents on their wedding day.

"Don't worry about it," my mom said to our contractor, Ed, after he apologized to her for the unplanned mess around the new patio. "Tell you what. If a couple of your guys could help me, let's just clean it up, dig up what little grass is left, rake it, and I'll plant a nice, big garden."

A garden. That's what she saw.

This area had a lot of wood lying in it. Broken bricks. Rocks.

Still, she saw a garden. A big one. Each side of the patio was a good twenty feet long. But within a couple of hours, Ed's guys had the area picked up and raked, the holes filled, and ready for plants.

And soon enough, my mom and I were at the local garden store to load up on plants. Keep in mind my mom had no practical knowledge about plants. She understood some liked sun and some liked shade. But that was really about the extent of her horticultural proficiency.

She had nothing particular in mind when we walked into the big humid greenhouse. She simply wanted lots of different flowers. She wanted color. As we strolled through the long aisles, she'd stop every so often to pick up a plant. She'd hold it with two hands, arms stretched out. She'd smell them. She'd smile at them. Some she picked. Some she didn't. I don't know why she chose the ones she did. I'm not sure she knew, either. I guess she simply followed her heart.

After we arrived home, we carried all of the plants to the new patio. It was the first time we could see all of our selections at once. We had a rainbow of color. And we also had what looked like a few hundred plants to get in the ground.

"What in the world are you doing?" came a voice from the garage. It was my dad. He had arrived home from work, and had obviously just got his first glimpse of us standing on the patio admiring our purchases.

Then began the bantering so typical between Mom and Dad.

"Hi! We're going to plant a garden!" answered my mom.

"Are you nuts? Do you realize how big that area is? Why don't we just put the grass back in?"

"We've got plenty of grass in our yard. We need some color out here."

"I think you're biting off more than you should. I think we should put grass in half of it."

"Well, we already bought all of the flowers. But if you want to make part of this grass, that's fine. I'll find a different spot in the backyard to put in another garden for the things that won't fit in here."

Amazing. My mom always could find the right words to say—in any situation. Never one to back down, she'd usually find a way to win through kindness. Gentleness. Or through words that were inarguable. I'm not sure I ever saw her persuasiveness lose.

"Fine," replied my dad. "If you want to plant them all here, go right ahead. But don't look to me when you're sick and tired of taking care of everything!"

With that, my dad shook his head and went into the house. The conversation was over. And my mom was the happy victor.

She smiled.

"OK, Jimmy, let's get working!"

My mom had no real approach to planting. She just started in. I, on the other hand, had to think out everything first. I had the plan; she had the spirit. We were a good team.

Our new garden had an abundance of flowers. Pink, yellow, orange, red, purple, white. Big flowers, fluffy flowers, delicate flowers, spiky flowers. We had a little bit of everything.

We finished planting the garden that night—long after the sun had set—under the faint light coming from a fixture near the back door of the garage.

We were covered with dirt. Our hands. Our faces. Our knees. Our clothes.

"We have such good soil here," my mom said to me. Then she proceeded to tell me about farming, about farmers, about her childhood relatives in central Nebraska and Iowa who farmed. She told me what soil was like in other parts of the country. She said it could be like clay. My mom could talk for a good fifteen minutes on any topic—including soil.

And, as usual, she wanted to make a point.

We had good soil under us.

PICKING THE ACTUAL date for my surgery wasn't quite as easy as I expected it to be.

After I finished my consultation with my doctor in his office, our only remaining business was to get surgery scheduled.

"Let's go up to the front desk to see when I have some slots open in the next month," he said.

I'm not exactly sure what I was expecting, but it was more than I got at the front desk. Alright, I guess deep down I thought I was suddenly very important and everyone involved in my upcoming surgery would now treat me kind of like a celebrity. I mean, come on, this was *big*!

"Where's the surgery calendar?" my doctor asked the front desk attendant.

"Don't ask me Dr. B, you had it last!" she shouted back.

They couldn't find the surgery calendar. This was not going well. So then my doctor pulled out a blank calendar he found on the front desk. It was a freebie from a pharmaceutical company. There was nothing on it. He proceeded then, to pencil in what he thought were his blackout dates over the next month.

"I'm on vacation this week. Oh yeah, isn't that conference on the eighteenth or nineteenth?"

My God! I thought. *How can he be talking about time off!*

After a minute or two of mental gymnastics on his part, he threw out four dates.

One was the following week. "Too soon," I said.

Two of the dates were three weeks out.

"Maybe," I said.

And one was a month away, May 26.

One would think I would be standing there prepared to say, "Hey, let's march over to the hospital right now. I'll strip down. You slice me open and cut until it's all gone."

I was weighing so many things. Work. Family. My own mental state. Secretly, I also wanted to attend something at our church I had been working on for a couple of weeks. It was nothing more than a big, parish-wide party. But I wanted to be there.

Joining this group—and agreeing to play a leadership role in it—was one of the many things I have done in my life where I simply followed my heart. I didn't really have the time to get involved with it. But my heart said yes. This was going to be a great party. A blue-ribbon celebration. And it had become a central part of my world in recent weeks.

I stood there in the doctor's office. I knew I had cancer, and I wanted it out of me. But I also had this very strong, conflicting feeling.

"Would I be crazy to wait until May 26?" I asked. "Would that be too big of a risk?"

He assured me waiting a month was not a problem.

"Put it in ink then," I told him. "May 26 it is."

The party became my distraction over the following weeks. Our planning committee had countless meetings, many of them at 6:00 AM on Saturdays at a local Denny's restaurant. I carried notebooks and files with me every waking minute so I could write down new ideas or plans. The details of the party consumed any time that wasn't spent thinking about the heaviness of cancer, surgery, and recovery.

The setup for the party started the day before the event. I love the bonding that takes place at moments like this. All of the planning and dreaming starts to evolve into realities. People magically show up to help.

But there also can come a time when there are too many "chefs" in the kitchen. That point had arrived, and I had no interest in getting involved. My work was done; I was ready for fun.

Barry, one of the other organizers of the event, felt the same way I did.

"You feel like getting out of here and pulling some weeds by the main entrance?" he asked me.

The weather was great outside. I looked at the chaos going on inside. Being outside sounded perfect. Weeding sounded perfect.

So, in the middle of all of this, Barry and I slipped away from the high-flying energy inside to work on something neither of us had ever considered. We started pulling weeds from the landscaped beds that flanked the sidewalk leading up to the church's main door.

And there were a LOT of weeds to pull, which gave us time to talk about a variety of topics.

We talked about our mutual excitement. We talked about how great it was to see people involved. We talked about a few minor things we would like to change. We talked about kids. Work. Life. Barry's beloved White Sox.

"Wouldn't it be awesome to surprise people with a bunch of bright red geraniums out here?" Barry said to me. Red was the official color of the party.

I had actually been thinking the exact, same thing.

"Let's do it! Great idea!" I said to him. And within an hour, we had made a round-trip excursion to our local hardware store to buy several flats of bright red geraniums.

Our party was now less than twenty-four hours away. Still faced with what seemed to be a list of endless tasks to accomplish, volunteers were starting to get frazzled. Yet Barry and I were quite content outside planting red geraniums.

Barry hollered over to ask me if I needed his spade.

Despite the rawness of the cold soil under my fingernails, which was intense, I shouted back, "No, the soil's actually pretty easy to work with. I'm surprised."

I sat there, kneeling on the hard concrete sidewalk. Barry was talking, but his words no longer registered with me. I was, once again, thinking about the events of the last several weeks. I replayed conversations. I remembered lines from e-mails and notes. I thought about my family.

I looked at my hands and was deeply aware of how alive I was. My senses were on overdrive.

And while I had spent weeks planning and working on this big, fun celebration, I knew what I would remember from the entire event was this one moment with Barry. Feeling dirt embedded under my fingernails.

I also thought of my mom and her lecture about soil.

Sure enough, she was right. We had good soil under us.

Lesson 10

Plant

yourself

in

good soil.

Chapter 11

That's Why They Call It Work

MY DAD BELIEVED in a number of things.

He believed in holding his five sons accountable for living up to some pretty high standards.

He believed he could never miss one of his children's athletic or school events. Never.

He believed the number "5" truly was his lucky number. Why else would God give him five sons? If he had to place a bet, you knew he would somehow work that number into the wager.

He believed in charity. Especially behind-the-scenes charity. I found this out when I learned, by accident, he had been paying the high school tuition for one of my brother's best friends for years. But

Above: My dad. Just like I remember him.

the school principal had to promise to keep my dad's identity as the benefactor a secret.

He believed in good grades.

He believed in playing hard.

He believed in respect and a host of other principles that established the framework for a loving, supportive family.

My dad's beliefs were simply a part of his DNA. They were not to be challenged or questioned.

The only thing I remember challenging my dad about was his belief I shouldn't have a serious summer job until I was a college student.

And that led to the only showdown I ever had with Dad.

I was finishing my senior year in high school and I wanted a summer job. I wanted to make some money for college. I begged him to let me apply for a position at a clothing store at our local mall. Or maybe wait tables at a restaurant. The options for summer work in my hometown were pretty limited, but I knew I could find something.

Anything.

But my dad dug in his heels. He simply didn't want me to have a summer job. His position made no sense to me. He had worked odd jobs throughout his youth. He was a newspaper boy. He delivered ice for ice coolers back in the "olden" days. He seemed to have an endless string of entertaining stories about the jobs he had held throughout his youth.

But he was not about to let me work.

"You'll be working the rest of your life," he told me. "Enjoy your summer."

I tried every possible angle with my dad to convince him otherwise. But he held firm.

"How much could you possibly make this summer, Jim?" he asked me.

I ran some quick numbers in my head and told him I could probably make $1,000 during the summer if I was lucky.

"And you know you have to pay taxes on that, right?"

"Uh, sure. I know that," I replied unconvincingly.

The next thing I knew, my dad was pulling out his checkbook and writing me a $1,000 check.

"Trust me on this," he said. "Enjoy your summer. Do this for me. You're going to be working the rest of your life. Have fun. You'll never regret it."

"Dad, you don't need to . . ." I started to protest.

He wouldn't let me finish my sentence.

"Just take it. Next summer you can work. And you can work every summer after that. But this summer, give yourself this gift. Make that your job."

I GRADUATED FROM college in June at the age of twenty-one. I moved to Chicago the week after graduation with what I thought was a job with a highly reputable architectural firm. However, the day I showed up for my first day of work—as scheduled—I learned my position had already been eliminated. Bummer.

But it was summertime. And I was in downtown Chicago. Life wasn't all that bad.

So, while I didn't have a job, I did have a very fun summer.

Much to my dad's relief, however, I secured a real job in September. And I never stopped working after that.

Consequently, by the time I had surgery, I had been working for twenty-two years, eight months, and fourteen days.

My dad was right. In the blink of an eye, I truly had been working the rest of my life.

During those last few days before surgery, I began to realize something as I was splitting up my work responsibilities and giving things away. I realized work truly had *become* my life. It *defined* me.

For years, I loved my career. And I loved the people I worked with. I was lucky. I was in the right place at the right time. I was fortunate to have others who constantly opened doors for me. I was paid more than I was worth. What more could I want?

But I really knew my heart wasn't in it any more.

I'd often tease that, in my next life, I wanted to be the guy at the beachside hut selling T-shirts and renting bikes to tourists. And I wanted to be a writer. People would always laugh, as would I. But the truth was I meant it. I wanted something different.

However, I learned how to suppress the inner voice speaking to me because there was always the lure of a paycheck around the corner.

There were so many things going through my head as my surgery rapidly approached. My career. My family. My priorities. My life.

What would I be remembered for?

Perhaps the gift Karen described to me was going to involve wrestling all of these issues down one at a time until they made sense. Maybe I'd come out on the other side with clear direction and purpose. My head was spinning.

It had been twenty-seven years since I was a high school graduate begging my dad to let me get that summer job.

Now, here I was, a forty-four-year-old man working through the reality of having my first entire summer off in years. I could still hear my dad's voice telling his seventeen-year-old son to enjoy his summer.

"Give yourself this gift. Make that your job."

My dad's words stirred something in me. Only this time around, they weren't an order.

They were words of wisdom.

Lesson 11

Work

isn't

everything.

Chapter 12

Summertime, and the Livin' Is Easy

SUMMER OFFICIALLY BEGINS on June 21. At least that's what the calendar states.

But for me, that's always been more of a technicality.

With my calendar, summer holds the firm time frame between Memorial Day and Labor Day.

When I was a kid in Nebraska, we had a cabin on a little lake about fifteen minutes from our house. We owned the cabin with two other families and took turns enjoying it following a prearranged schedule that our parents set up at the beginning of each summer. However, we

---

Above: The summer sun setting on our lake.

always celebrated Memorial Day and Labor Day together. All twenty-something of us.

Our Memorial Day bash was the official opening of the summer season. We'd pull our little speedboat out of storage, haul out all of the swimming toys and life jackets, rake down the sand on the beach, and air out the cabin as all of us—pale from the winter—celebrated the beginning of yet another hot Nebraska summer. For us children, who had typically finished the last day of school in the prior week, it was our first opportunity to taste the freedom of summer.

This was not a fancy cabin. It had two bedrooms, the coolest of which had bunk beds. It had a big patio facing the lake, and a long, sloping sandy beach. And all of the furnishings were a mishmash of old relics from the three families.

Three months after our Memorial Day bash, we were back together again, this time at our Labor Day party. More relaxed and tanned than we had been on Memorial Day, we enjoyed one more final hurrah before we returned to school, studies, and schedules.

In between those two parties, we welcomed a life that slowed down.

We had a revolving door of friends and families out to the cabin.

We took time for each other.

We grilled.

We played board games.

We hung out.

My brothers seemed to tolerate me more. Sometimes, I even thought they liked me.

My dad was more playful.

Our dog ran loose.

We kept the windows open at night and could hear the steady sound of trains on nearby tracks.

We did this every year.

Enjoying the sounds, the tastes, the smells, the sights, and the feel of summer.

THE ONLY GOOD thing about surgery—if it's possible to say that—was waking up afterward. At first, I wasn't even sure if the operation was over or if I was about to go into surgery. And there was a brief moment, as I recall, of assessment to ascertain if I was dead. Things were very foggy. But I remember being aware of heaviness throughout my body. It was quiet. I couldn't move from my waist down. My legs felt as if an elephant was sitting on them.

I moved my hands slowly down to my abdomen. Tubes were attached everywhere. Aisle five of Ace Hardware had apparently been relocated to my stomach.

Yep. I was in the recovery room.

I had a nurse named Brian. I had no sense of any other person in my life. Just Brian.

I went in and out of the most relaxing sleep. I thought about nothing. I simply existed.

Such was my pattern for hours and hours. Exist. Sleep. Wake. Think of nothing. Repeat.

The lights were dim. I could feel a perfect breeze. I heard equipment humming.

I was content. I was at peace with the world. I was at peace with myself. I didn't know anything about the outcome of my surgery. I didn't need or want to ask. And while the anesthesia was doing the lion's share of the work to keep me in this state, I also was fairly clear about what was registering in my mind.

I visualized I had arrived at the other side. The other side of just *what*, exactly, I wasn't sure. But I had this strong sensation I had ascended to the top of a mountain and I could now start to see what was on the other side.

As groggy and foggy as I was on the outside, my soul had clarity it had never experienced before.

Around ten o'clock that night, I was moved to a room—in the pediatric ward.

How hilariously appropriate, I thought.

And I had the most wonderfully peaceful night's sleep.

Paradisiac.

When I woke the next morning, I was alone, and I lay in my room and thought.

Not about surgery, however. I also didn't think about what the doctor might tell me that day.

Instead, I realized it was the Friday before Memorial Day. The Memorial Day weekend was starting. And I was going to be in the hospital through all of it.

No projects to complete. No chores to do. No schedules.

The Memorial Day weekend was here and I was going to do something I hadn't done in a long, long time.

Absolutely nothing.

And even though it wasn't yet June 21, summer had finally returned.

Lesson 12

Rest.

Chapter 13

Here Comes Santa Claus

IT WAS OUR last Christmas in North Carolina. Kevin was eight, and Wallis was five. That would make Drew a one-year-old, newly mastering the art of walking. It was the week before Christmas, and our good friends, David and Denise, had invited us over to their home, along with two other families, for a kid-friendly Christmas celebration.

Among our four families, we had ten little kids—with Kevin being the oldest. While we were transplants to the area, the other families were all natives. Southern to the bone.

I love Christmas in the south. I love celebrating Christmas with southerners. They masterfully blend the richness of formality with the warmth of tradition. And while I will always love the smell of the

Nebraska evergreens that draped our mantel when I was a kid, I've grown to appreciate the beauty of a southern mantel adorned with magnolia leaves. (And I even learned the glistening glow on the leaves comes from a special mayonnaise rubbing.)

So here we were, with our adopted southern friends, enjoying the warmth of a roaring fire and the smell of cinnamon-apple cider on the stove.

The kids played games and sipped their drinks out of fancy, glass Christmas mugs, while the parents guarded every sip to ensure that not a drop of the holiday juice ended up on their velvety best. Kevin ran around, his shirt untucked, with two fistfuls of peanuts. Wallis, with her long, flowing hair, quietly smiled—absorbing everything that was taking place. And Drew stuffed his cheeks with crackers, remembering to swallow every so often.

It was, indeed, the perfect party.

And then, the perfect party got even MORE perfect!

"What's that?" exclaimed our host, David, to all of the children. "Did anyone hear bells?"

Bells? Even the adults looked a little curious and tried to figure out what David was talking about.

"There it is again," he said. "I think I hear bells out back!"

Instantly, every child scurried to the sliding glass doors at the back of the house, pushing their frosting-covered faces to the windows—desperately trying to see into the darkness beyond. Wondering. About bells. And the possibility of . . .

Ding-Dong!

Now ten pairs of little feet went scurrying to the *front* door.

Ten pairs of eyes. Wide open.

And then it happened. David opened the front door.

"Ho, Ho, Ho!"

It was Santa! It was Santa! Apparently, he and his reindeer had just flown in from the North Pole. So while the reindeer rested in the backyard, Santa was going to enjoy some time with us!

And then Santa, after finding the perfect chair to plop his tired body in, did something I will never forget. He patiently took the children, one-by-one, sat each one on his lap, and talked to them. He conversed with them. Individually. For a good five to ten minutes each. And these weren't talks centered on what each child wanted to find in his or her stocking. (Although Wallis managed to get in her request for a new stuffed teddy bear!) Santa *talked* to the boys and girls—*with* each child—about their lives, their hopes, and their dreams.

Santa listened. Santa cared. And Santa gave them reason to believe. In everything. Including themselves.

While the adults attempted to do typical grown-up things like clear dishes and tie shoelaces, we were all taken aback by Santa. He wasn't the typical white-bearded, rotund man in a red suit we were accustomed to seeing at the mall. His beard looked pretty darn real. When he bent down to pick up the next child, you could see his long underwear, which didn't look like anything you could purchase in our neck of the woods.

"He's amazing," I whispered to David. "Thanks."

"We didn't do anything," was his only reply.

Something magical was taking place.

After the children took turns with our visitor from the North Pole, Santa then talked to us as a group. He told us about his wife, about his life, and about how happy he was to be with us.

And then, sadly, he told us he needed to leave because he still had other families to visit that night. The children took their turns hugging Santa good-bye. So did the adults.

And then Santa stepped into the darkness of the backyard as he called out to the reindeer.

The last thing we heard was the sound of sleigh bells in the distant loblolly pines of our friends' backyard.

On our short drive home, with the three children in the backseat of the car, not one of us spoke a word, until . . .

"There's Santa!" exclaimed an excited Kevin who was peering out the backseat window.

And as I pulled the car over to the side of the road so we could all look, I saw what Kevin saw. A flashing red light moving slowly through the Carolina sky. Moving from right to left. Blink. Blink. Blink.

A typical observer might have thought it was the Duke University Life Flight helicopter.

But not my children.

"I see Rudolf!" exclaimed Wallis.

Drew tried to wiggle out of his car seat to see.

I looked up in the sky at the blinking red light moving silently through the moonlit night. Then I looked back and saw my three children gazing up at the world above them. Eyes bulging. Mouths open.

"See you next week, Santa!" Kevin yelled out.

I looked back again at the kids and realized this moment had little to do with what they saw.

It had everything to do with what they believed.

ONCE I LEFT the recovery room and my best friend forever, nurse Brian, I quickly made a new BFF for the next four days. My morphine drip.

I have never had a friend so loyal, so comforting, and so gosh-darn great to be around. My new BFF never left my bedside, took care of me around the clock, and helped ease every worry that might have consumed my usually overactive brain. Considering all I had been through, things were pretty euphoric.

So euphoric that the sensation I had in the recovery room—that feeling of being on top of a mountain and looking out toward the world beyond—continued throughout most of my hospital stay. And when the morphine was working overtime, I'd sometimes enjoy visits from flying dragons, a flock of geese, and a group of pointy-eared folks who would stand on top of my television.

I can't say I recall many other details those first couple of postsurgical days.

I do recall, certainly, my doctor coming to talk to me in my pediatric room the morning following surgery. I kept hearing him say the words "lymph nodes" over and over again thinking he was trying to share bad news with me.

Ultimately, I realized he was giving me positive news about my lymph nodes. They appeared clean. As did everything he could visually observe. We'd have to wait for the pathology report to really understand if my cancer had spread beyond the prostate.

In the meantime, he left me alone with my new friend.

I spent most of my days in the hospital quite content. I didn't sit and obsess about things. As best as I can recall, I simply enjoyed the tranquility and view of the world inside my head.

After a few days, much to my dismay, they kicked me out of the hospital. I actually asked if I could stay one more day, but according to my health insurance provider, it was time to leave. And leaving meant saying good-bye to my BFF.

And hello to a big bottle of painkillers. I also got my first real introduction to the body I was now attached to—held together with staples and sporting some new, temporary add-ons to my plumbing system. Suddenly, living minute to minute was a struggle.

Once I was home, everything was difficult. The pillow was in the wrong place. I couldn't reach a blanket. I was hot. I was cold. I was sweaty. I was constipated. I couldn't sit up. I couldn't reach the remote control. I didn't want to talk on the phone.

And truthfully, the panoramic view I thought was so stunning back in the pediatric ward was now looking more like a big, vast horizon with nothing but unreachable dreams.

The second day home, my doctor called to go over the findings from my pathology report. That didn't help how I was feeling. The cancer was far more invasive than he could see visually during the surgery.

"You have a very aggressive cancer that was on a path to kill you," I remember him saying. "But your margins are questionably close so they aren't sure if the cancer has spread."

All I could imagine was more surgery. Radiation. Or both. I realized, at that moment, I hadn't thought about the postoperative realities.

"So what do we do?" I asked.

"I'm not sure, Jim. We don't need to address that today. For now, you heal. You're coming out of a big surgery. Let's let your body mend, and then we'll run more tests to see if there is any indication of cancer cells. But for now, rest and heal," he told me.

I was frustrated. I wasn't expecting that kind of outcome. I was expecting resolution so I could move forward. Physical pain and emotional stress—at the same time—are a weighty combination. I was sinking.

Fortunately, my son Kevin gave me a firm slap in the face.

He was talking to me about music. Specifically, he was talking about some song lyrics that moved him.

They were from a song titled "Sunny Hours" by the Long Beach Dub Allstars, and in typical Kevin style, he started singing. I'm not sure what I loved more, his voice or the one particular line that meant so much to him.

". . . never count the gloomy hours, I let them slip away . . ."

"You and I are exactly the same, Dad," Kevin said to me. "Don't you think?"

I looked at him and pondered his youthful wisdom. Clearly, there is a long bridge between the world of a teenage boy and his father. But Kevin's question to me hit home.

Who, exactly, was I? I had always been a person who believed. I believed in people. I believed in my feelings. I believed in a purpose and a reason for everything—good or bad—in life. I believed in my abilities. I believed in a person's word.

And I believed in myself.

Kevin's observation came when I most needed it. I needed to believe.

Not a blind belief that all would be dandy and we'd soon be singing around the campfire in a few weeks. It was a belief grounded in strength, with unwaivering faith that everything I was encountering had a purpose. Equally important was a belief that I had the inner strength to walk through whatever fires were ahead.

Kevin's message to believe was as powerful as the one Karen had given me a few weeks before.

Maybe they were connected?

Lesson 13

The first step

to

achieving

is

believing.

Chapter 14

Lifeguard on Duty

MY CLOSEST FRIEND in high school was Sid.

His family moved to my town the summer before our junior year in high school. Sid and I met on the first day of school and clicked instantly.

Sid was fun. He was adventurous. He had curly hair and the whitest teeth of any human I'd ever known. He also had the biggest smile and an infectious laugh.

Sid was also a swimmer. He had a swimmer's build, a swimmer's tan, and a swimmer's carefree attitude.

So, he pretty much was everything I was not.

Above: My wise friend, Sid. The lifeguard.

Sid exposed me to things that were totally foreign. His father owned a car dealership, so we often would hang out there doing odd jobs like washing cars or running errands to other dealerships.

Sid drove a Jeep. And I spent hundreds of hours as his passenger driving around and talking.

He had an intense passion for everything in his life. He also brought a simplistic insight to the many issues bouncing around our teenage heads.

Sid was the first friend I had whom I considered wise. He was an observer of life and people and I could always count on him to cut to the chase and bring a realistic and practical perspective to any situation.

He was also the first peer of mine to ever ask me what it was like to lose my mother.

"So, what's it like to have your mom die?" he asked me out of the blue one day.

No friend of mine, other than Sid, could have traveled with me for the next two hours as I shared things with him I didn't even understand myself.

It was a rite of passage for me in many ways because that was the first time I experienced the depth of a friend's compassion. Even a sixteen-year-old friend.

The summer after we graduated from high school, Sid was the head lifeguard at a local pool. It was the perfect job—for him, and for me because I'd hang out there most days.

And because I didn't have a job of my own, I'd help out whenever I was needed. I learned how to check the water chemistry and clean the filters. I became pretty proficient in using the skimmer bag to clean off the top of the water, too. I quickly learned all the mundane aspects of pool maintenance.

I also learned what it meant to be a lifeguard.

Sid was about to enter the University of Nebraska in Lincoln and I was about to move to Seattle to enroll in the University of Washington.

While my school didn't start until the middle of September, Sid had to leave for school around the third week of August, leaving the pool short a lifeguard for about three weeks until the last day of the season, which was Labor Day.

"Jim, you gotta be the lifeguard," Sid begged.

Me? Lifeguard?

I wasn't lifeguard material. I was just the lifeguard's sidekick.

But somehow it happened. I became a lifeguard, if only for a few weeks.

I was really excited on the first day on the job. I had a new yellow bathing suit and thought I was at least doing a respectable job of looking like a lifeguard.

More than anything, I was prepared for fun in the sun.

Until the second day on duty, that is. That would be the day Chuck, a family friend who was probably six or seven years old, appeared on the diving board early that memorable afternoon.

I hadn't recalled seeing Chuck in the deep end of the pool during the summer. But I was sure he wouldn't be on the diving board if he shouldn't be there.

He wouldn't do anything stupid, I thought to myself.

So, I waved to him as he jumped.

And Chuck smiled at me with his toothless smile. He was still smiling as he went under the water.

And under the water he stayed.

No more than ten seconds elapsed from the time Chuck jumped off the diving board to the time I pulled him from the bottom of the pool. I couldn't even think fast enough to use any of the lifesaving skills I had learned in my lifeguarding crash course a couple weeks earlier.

"Chuck, what were you thinking!" I screamed at his no-longer-smiling face.

"I dunno. Am I in trouble?"

Funny. I was asking the same question of myself at that moment.

And it was at exactly that moment that being a lifeguard took on a whole new meaning for me.

———————————————

THE MAJORITY OF my healing after surgery took place outside by our pool.

I'd wake up most days, put on a bathing suit, and basically hang out poolside as much as possible. Aside from having had my insides Roto-Rootered, and a few tubes hanging off of me, you'd think I was enjoying a resort getaway in the Riviera. The truth was, the sun felt incredible.

Building this pool a few years earlier was either the dumbest thing I had ever done or the smartest. I had rationalized putting it in by convincing myself I'd use it to swim laps.

The laps lasted about a week.

But the pool quickly became the centerpiece of our family life. It's where everyone would congregate throughout the craziness of our days.

Over the years, while my sons and daughter could often be found *in* the pool with friends, I was the one who tended to walk *around* the pool in a bathing suit. Patrolling. Throwing stray balls back into the water. Tinkering with the pool equipment. Testing the water. Watching.

I became, in actuality, the lifeguard. After all, I had a certificate!

After surgery, my poolside perch also became the hangout for the nightly army of friends who brought dinner to our family for weeks.

This became an instrumental part of my healing. Not the food. The people.

Virtually every afternoon, late in the day, I'd get to see someone different. Some days it might be people who were part of our family's inner circle. Other days—most days, in fact—it would be people who were casual acquaintances. Maybe from church. Friends of friends. Neighbors who lived two blocks down and three houses in. They were the people in all of our lives who we had passed by knowingly without allowing any kind of connection.

But cancer helps break down those barriers.

"Come on, sit down. Join us!" I'd say to them after thanking them for their culinary kindness.

Almost every one of them sat. And almost every one of them, I could tell, had squeezed the "Higley Dinner" into a very busy personal schedule.

And almost every one of them stayed for longer than the initial time frame they had allowed themselves.

"Just a few minutes" turned into twenty.

"Ten minutes" transformed into forty-five.

"I don't want to intrude" became a second glass of wine, dinner, and a call to the rest of their family to come over for a swim.

They brought food to nourish and fill us. But what they ultimately brought was so much more.

They brought us the nourishment of themselves. They simply needed to be asked. For me, having the chance to stop and talk with people was such an enlightening part of my summer. It was my daily reminder that everyone has a story. Hardships. Pain. Everyone. Yet, somehow we are all intrinsically connected to each other in very tangible ways.

These people seasoned my days with their stories. They warmed my heart with their own struggles. They gave me ziplock bags of compassion. And they prepared those ingredients in a slow cooker. Not in a microwave.

And in doing so, they not only were our chefs for a day.

They became something far more valuable.

They were our lifeguards.

Lesson 14

Lifeguards

are

always

on duty.

Chapter 15

Will You Sign My Yearbook?

THE BEST THING about the last day of school as a junior high student was receiving a yearbook.

Sure, report cards were also handed out that day. But it was the yearbook everyone looked forward to getting. The yearbook, in many ways, became the defining moment as to whether the school year would be remembered as a good one or not.

Job one, when you received your yearbook, had to be done quickly and discreetly. This was the "flip-through-every-page-as-fast-as-you-can" move to ascertain how many times your picture could be found.

Above: Kevin, Wallis, and Drew. All in braces. As they looked during my summer of healing.

While nobody would admit it, we all had a rating scale for ourselves as to "how we did." Mine went something like this:

- **I'M DISAPPOINTED BUT I CAN COPE:** The only picture of me in the yearbook was my class picture. That's it. Nothing else.

- **I'M EMBARRASSED. SHOOT ME NOW:** The only picture of me in the yearbook was my class picture. And I look like a nerd. My life is over.

- **HONORABLE MENTION:** I've got the class picture. And it's OK. I'm also in one or more pictures of clubs or teams I had joined. No complaints.

- **HOME RUN:** I've got the class picture and it's good. I'm in one or more pictures of clubs or teams. Best of all, I'm in a candid shot. If it's just me, that's fine. If it's me with friends, well, my year couldn't get any better.

Yearbooks were important. You could look at your yearbook and take pride in things you never took the time to think about throughout the year. It gave you a chance to step back and see the world you were communed with and begin to comprehend a little bit about who you were.

Beyond the pictures found on every page, there was one thing I loved more than anything about yearbooks. One thing that had more meaning, more insight, and more value.

It was the handwritten words, from classmates and teachers on that last day of school, as we passed our books around for each other to sign.

I was always excited to read the comments my friends made. I was even more excited to read the comments the girls I had long-standing crushes on would write.

My good friends always came through as expected. Some were better than others. Some were funny. Some were serious. But they all sounded like true-blue friends.

The girls were a mixed bag. Most were total letdowns. A few were nice. And every once in a while I'd get one that totally confused me.

Some of the things people wrote were downright flattering.

- "To a super nice kid . . ."
- "You're a guy who's almost perfect. Don't get stuck up."
- "Jim, you are a great guy and have the best attitude towards life."
- "You're one of the nicest persons I know . . ."

Good stuff to read when you're fourteen years old or so. But then again, those are the kind of comments you expect to read from your good friends. That was where the surprise came in. Some of these comments came from people I didn't know that well. And their words always made me stop and reflect.

I loved the tradition of signing yearbooks. I assumed everyone did. It was the one time of the year you could let down your guard and speak from your heart. It was the one time of the year you could write anything to anyone.

I've lost many a report card. I've tossed many a class project. But I hold on to every single yearbook.

I keep them not just for the pictures. I keep them for those written words from friends and people I never knew were my friends.

I keep them because those words—quite simply—remind me who I was to the people in my life.

IF YOU WERE to map my movement with a GPS during those first couple of postsurgical weeks, you'd see a big, black blob directly over my house. I didn't move too far from home.

One of my favorite daily journeys took place every afternoon between 2:00 and 3:00. It was my slow, steady walk out to our curbside mailbox and back.

Sure, generally speaking, mail isn't something most people look forward to. Catalogs, promotional postcards, flyers, and, of course, bills usually make up most of the mail I've received over most of my adult life.

But one of the perks of being sick or having surgery is that you start receiving cards and notes. And most days during that summer at home brought me someone's well wishes or thoughts.

I got used to it really fast.

The sound of our mailman's well-worn muffler huffing and puffing down the street was my sign to head out to retrieve the day's catch. My ritual was the same. I'd flip through the pile of envelopes as I walked up our driveway back to the house and take a mental inventory of the envelopes and return addresses. It wasn't unusual to find one from someone who wasn't a part of my world—sometimes even a total stranger. Those were the envelopes I'd always dig into first. Partially out of curiosity. Partially because it was interesting to learn what would prompt people to take time and send a card.

Day after day, I'd think to myself, "How cool was that?"

I'd also think about how exceedingly simple it is to do something nice. I'd feel good. And I'd also feel a little guilty because I was regularly reminded of how often in my life I've failed to do something thoughtful for another person. I used to do those things.

I'd also think about an article I read years earlier in the *Chicago Tribune*. It was written by columnist Mary Schmich. Her words originally had such an impact on me I cut out the article and pinned it to my bulletin board at work. And over the years, the article yellowed and picked up several more pinholes in it as I moved it around my bulletin board. But her message never aged.

She wrote about a colleague of hers, Jeff MacNelly, a Pulitzer Prize–winning editorial cartoonist who had been fighting lymphoma.

She wrote about how, for several months, she had a yellow Post-it note on her desk that reminded her to "Write Jeff." She wrote about how she'd write other notes here and there to remind her to drop Jeff a note. She wrote about how she would often think of Jeff and how much she missed seeing him. And she wrote about how, as opposed to writing Jeff at those moments, she would just write herself another note to remind herself to write Jeff.

She shared what eventually moved her to take the few minutes to write him. She had heard that things were not good.

So she finally wrote him a quick note and put it in the mail.

In her column, she wrote about why she never took the time to write him prior to that day. It was simply because she didn't know what to say.

"So, for lack of the perfect thing to say, I said the worst thing possible—nothing."

Her note never reached her friend. He died a day after she mailed it.

I received a variety of cards and notes that summer. Some were humorous. Some serious. Some religious. Some homemade. Some simply had signatures. Others had lengthy notes.

I valued each one equally.

Words truly can heal. They can surprise. They can encourage. It doesn't matter if they are handwritten or if Hallmark had to be leaned on for a little help.

Words matter.

Because they remind each of us who we are to the people in our lives.

Lesson 15

Say it.

Write it.

Today.

Chapter 16

Ob-la-di, Ob-la-da, Life Goes On

IT WAS THE second or third week in May.

I was forty. My brother Kevin was forty-six.

It was a day like most days except this was one of the last days Kevin lived. And I had the joy of living it with him.

Over the prior eighteen months, I had made numerous trips to Denver to be with Kevin—as did all of my brothers. We grabbed a day or two as often as we could. I'd arrange my visits around "business trips," but there was very little business going on. These trips were all about Kevin. They were about sneaking away and submerging into Kevin's world as often as possible.

Above: My brother Kevin. Always with a camera in hand.

Each trip gave me vivid memories; this particular visit in May, however, seemed to encapsulate all that was Kevin. It helped me bring closure—in part—to the relationship Kevin and I had experienced on earth. During this visit, Kevin gave me a gift that would become forever etched in my heart. And I saw Kevin for the very last time.

I found him in his family room watching the news on television when I woke up my first morning there. I was still wearing the clothes I had slept in. He was dressed. His wife had already left for work, so we had the house to ourselves.

"I need you to take me to the mall today," he said slowly and kindly when I walked into the room. "I want to check out that new Beatles CD."

Kevin was a huge Beatles fan for as long as I can recall. Growing up, I used to sneak looks at his collection of Beatles albums (which I was absolutely forbidden to do) to check out the funny haircuts and funny clothes on those four guys from a faraway place called Liverpool.

When I had arrived the day before, Kevin had mentioned something about this new CD—a collection of some important songs.

"And don't go telling anyone we're doing this."

I couldn't imagine how I was going to get Kevin to the mall. He could barely walk. He shuffled. Slowly. Getting him to and from the bathroom in his home was an undertaking. He wouldn't use a wheelchair, either, so a public outing sounded impossible.

But I knew we were going to try.

He guided me to a mall fifteen or twenty minutes from his home. There I was driving a car, my brother sitting next to me inside the body of a ninety-year-old man. Feeble. Tired. But not yet beaten.

I maneuvered the car as close to the main entrance as I could. There was a bench about twenty feet away we both spotted.

"Why don't you drop me off here and then go park the car," he said somewhat apologetically in his gentle voice. "I think I can get to that bench myself and then I'll wait for you."

"You bet, Kevin. That's great." I tried to sound encouraging. I wanted so badly to make this happen for him because he rarely asked for anything.

After I helped Kevin get out at the curb, I parked the car and ran back to him as fast as I could.

He hadn't progressed a dozen feet.

"Just walk next to me, Jim. In case I need to hold on to you."

By the time we made our way through the mall doors, Kevin suggested we go into the Barnes and Noble near the entrance and get something to drink.

"Sounds perfect, Kevin," I replied. What I was *really* thinking was how relieved I was *not* to have to get Kevin through the entire mall at that moment.

Every table was empty when we inched our way into the bookstore but we still picked a spot a little out-of-the-way. I got myself a cup of coffee and a glass of water for Kevin. His taste buds weren't working, he told me.

What was working, however, was his ability to share from his heart. And what Kevin chose to share with me that day was what it meant to him to be a photographer.

Kevin's business was print photography. Newspapers. Magazines. He covered the entire spectrum of life. Sports, current events, politics, and human interest. He did it all.

And he did it in a way that was so very Kevin.

I loved seeing Kevin's pictures, especially when they were in a newspaper with his name in the byline. My favorite photographs were of the "everyday" person. The guy next door.

I always suspected those were Kevin's favorite subjects too.

Our conversation confirmed that hunch. He shared with me in detail what it was like to photograph these people. He talked about how nervous they often were. And how he learned to take his time with them.

When his subject was a celebrity, an athlete or a politician, he would typically have a short window of time in which to shoot a sufficient number of poses and get his job done. So he knew how to move fast.

But with everyone else, he had a different approach.

He would show up at their door empty-handed. No camera, no notebook. Nothing. Just himself.

He would hang out with them—in their environment, in their world. And he would do what came so naturally to him.

Talk.

He showed interest in every person he was photographing. Interest in their story. He said he would always endeavor to find something in his life he could relate to in their world. He told me what it was like to connect with the 100-year-old man with thirty-nine great-grand-children. And the kid who caught a twenty-two-inch-long frog. Or the grandma who won the county yodeling contest.

And he wouldn't go back to his car to get his camera until he felt he had earned a person's trust. For, at that point, he could simply continue the conversation with the individual and shoot away without them feeling any anxiety or stress.

In the newspaper business, you live by deadlines—tight ones, usually. Kevin talked to me about how he had learned over the years to perform his job without letting deadlines run his life. Or lessen his experience. He talked about how he tried never to let other people know what his deadlines were. He talked about balance.

He talked about all the stories he would have missed had he solely focused on his deadlines.

He talked slowly. Sometimes he would stop and sit and look at me. For seconds at a time. Sometimes he would close his eyes, and I would watch him breathe. I imagined him seeing all these people in the photo album of his mind. Each and every one of them.

His stories were a little random, but his message was crystal clear. Time has value. What we do with our time—even when there are deadlines—is a choice.

"Let's go to the music store," he said as if he suddenly was done looking at his photo album and ready to run a race.

I looked at my watch. We had been in Barnes and Noble almost three hours. It felt like it had been thirty minutes.

In the music store, Kevin befriended a young clerk and inquired about the Beatles CD. Sure enough, it hadn't been released yet.

"Another month or two," the clerk said.

Then, the two of them started a conversation, which led to the topic of guitars. This young man was an aspiring musician. He made extra money playing in coffee houses on weekends. Kevin could play the guitar. Not fabulously well. But well enough to help him have a good conversation about the experience with this young man.

At one point, looking at his own watch, the clerk said to Kevin, "Hey, man, give me your phone number and I'll call you when we get the CD in."

"Tell you what," Kevin said, "I might not be in town next month. But I'll try to stop back in again."

"Cool," the clerk said smiling.

I looked at Kevin and felt as if I would burst into tears. My brother, my middle-of-the-night-baby-bottle-delivery-boy brother, was making sure I had one last lesson for the road.

If ever there was a man with a deadline, I was looking at him. If ever there was a man who had the right to announce his deadline to the world it was him.

But you'd never know it.

Even without a camera hanging around his neck that day, Kevin was still a master of his craft.

And his own time.

"**JIM, IT'S JACK.** I'm calling to check in on you and see how surgery went."

I had known Jack for eight years at that point. His two sons, Taylor and Mitch, had been good friends of Kevin and Wallis for many years. Their family was a regular fixture in our lives.

After a nice, friendly talk on the phone, Jack asked me if I might be up for going on a walk sometime.

"Absolutely," I quickly answered. "But I'm moving pretty slow right now."

Jack was an easy guy to be around. I've been to many parties in his home. He and his wife have been in our home numerous times as well. I've sat through ballgames with him. I've been to graduation ceremonies with him. We've carpooled with each other more times than I can count. But even though Jack was a familiar person in my life, it dawned on me how little I knew about him.

"Terrific. How about next Wednesday?" Jack replied.

"What time?"

"Oh, I don't know. I'll get up and go to the gym. I'll come over after that."

"Um, great. I'll be here. See you then!"

He picked me up that following Wednesday. And for many Wednesdays thereafter.

Our walks grew longer with each passing week as my pace became faster. And during those walks, we talked. Not solely about the weather or our kids.

We truly talked. Jack unknowingly became my therapist.

Jack had had a flourishing career with a healthcare company for more than twenty years. Over the years, he witnessed buyouts and mergers and countless reorganizations. During that time, he ascended the corporate ladder.

He enjoyed the respect of his peers and had financial success.

He survived layoffs. He saw the company culture change. And he ultimately saw his own enthusiasm for his career wane.

"I couldn't keep doing it, Jim," he told me. "If I did, I realized I was cheating not only my company but also my associates."

So he left. Walked away.

And before the age of fifty, he gave himself a gift—the gift of rediscovering himself.

He had no road map. No preset plan.

He simply knew it was time.

Every week I listened to him tell me the story of his journey. And I was inspired.

Inspired to look at my own life. Inspired to look at where I had been, where I was, and where I had the potential to go.

I looked forward every week to my time with Jack. I was convinced his message was part of the gift I was searching for.

But his message also stirred a lot of conflict within me. It was easy to soak in his inspiration, but he wasn't there with answers. I wanted answers!

That wasn't his purpose.

I'd go back to his well of wisdom week after week trying to find that answer. But there never was one.

He just kept planting the question.

Lesson 16

Life flies.

Watch

your time.

Chapter 17

I Wish They All Could Be California Girls

COULD LIFE BE any better for a teenage boy from Nebraska than to spend a couple of weeks each summer hanging out with his relatives in California?

I got to do that every year from the age of fourteen until I was nearly out of college as part of my annual pilgrimage to visit my favorite relatives, the "California" Higleys.

To be more specific, that would be my Uncle Jack, who was my dad's oldest brother; his wife, Aunt Margaret; and my three cousins, John, Linda, and Pam.

They lived in Southern California; thus, Disneyland, Knotts Berry Farm, and the Pacific Ocean were all at their fingertips. They had a

Above: Pam. Me. Under the California sun.

ping-pong table in their garage, they drank from a bottled water dispenser in their kitchen, and they wore cool clothes.

They were totally *not* like anyone from Nebraska.

When my brothers and I were youngsters, we'd go out to visit them every couple of years. And they'd begrudgingly come to Nebraska every several years—usually over Christmas, when we were having a record-breaking snowstorm. It's no wonder they all thought living in the Midwest was stupid.

Bottom line, we saw them a lot.

Uncle Jack was a banker. I always thought he looked like Jack Benny. He wasn't anything like my dad. He enjoyed the arts. Theater. Gardening. He seemed far more adventurous than my dad.

Aunt Margaret was the perfect aunt. Straight out of central casting. A Canadian. Tall. Always had something on her mind. And, she taught me how to eat artichokes.

Actually she *forced* me to eat artichokes.

"Jimmy," she'd say, "you need to expand your horizons!"

I thought I'd barf. But for her I'd try anything.

John, the oldest, was the exact same age as my twin brothers. But he seemed much nicer (meaning he talked to me) than my brothers ever were.

Linda was my brother Kevin's age. She was smart. She played the violin. A little quiet, she was nevertheless the first person I ever knew who made me feel like I was interesting.

That left Pam. Pam was one year my senior. I don't ever remember *not* knowing Pam. She and I always had an unspoken bond as children. She was the sister I never had, and I was the little brother she never had.

After my mom died, my dad sent me out to spend a couple of weeks with "Uncle Jack" every summer. Was he doing it for me or did he need a break from his teenage son? Probably a little of both. He got no complaints from me.

I loved going to California in the summer.

While I was there, I always did the same thing. I tagged along with

Pam. Everywhere she'd go.

I'd follow her to the beach. I'd go to with her to get haircuts. I'd visit her friends. I'd tag along on dates. I'd crash her friends' parties.

Pam and I have always had a relationship where we could step in and out of each other's lives—be it two months or two years—and pick up where we last left off.

My summer visits to California were cathartic. Aunt Margaret was devastated by my mother's death, and she went to great lengths to love me, comfort me, and give me all the mothering she could. Uncle Jack and I had similar interests, so we always had fun doing things that were new and exciting too.

But my visits really centered on Pam. And getting a tan.

Every year I'd tell Pam, "This is the year for a good tan!"

And every year, the story turned out the same.

We'd carefully work on a tanning program. We'd schedule our days around the sun. Pam would provide me with different lotions, oils, and other products to enhance a deep, bronze tan.

And every year, about two days before I was scheduled to fly home, I'd start to peel. It always started with an innocent mark on my shoulder or my forehead. I'd think it was nothing. But it was something. It was the beginning of a full-fledged snakeskin peel. And by the time I would board the plane home to Nebraska, I looked more like a leper than a boy who had just spent two weeks basking in the California sun.

Pam would laugh. I'd be upset. So she would laugh more.

I never got a good tan. But I did carry that California warmth back to Nebraska every year.

"TELL ME WHAT I can do. I'll do anything."

Those were the words I heard from Pam when I told her about my surgery.

Pam was one of the very few people in my life who, when they presented me with that question, I actually had a real answer in mind. And it wasn't my "I'm registered!" story.

But I had to pause. My first reaction wasn't to tell her what I needed from her. She's a mom with three kids. She's got a busy life in California. She is also the yin to my yang.

"Really, Jim. Anything."

Was I taking advantage of an emotional situation? I quickly debated with myself. Pam's mom, my Aunt Margaret, had died a few months earlier. It crushed Pam. And my cancer was Pam's second blow.

Oh, what the hell, I thought to myself before I blurted out what my heart was telling me.

"Pam, I need you to come here and just hang out. I need something to look forward to. And I need someone to make me laugh. That's what I need."

There. I had said it. I had asked her. I had laid the big one out there.

She had simply a one-word response: "When?"

Within a couple of hours, she was booked on a flight to come out a few weeks after my surgery. I loved knowing Pam was out there—on my healing horizon—and hopefully at a time when I would be well on the road to recovery. I wanted to look forward to belly laughs without blowing stitches.

As if looking forward to seeing her wasn't enough, the anticipation got even better when she called me the week before my surgery with a surprise. "Jim, Dad wants to come with me. He needs to see you. Can you handle that?"

At the age of eighty-seven, and recently widowed, my Uncle Jack needed to see me?

I said yes. An unequivocal yes!

I knew I needed Pam. And now that the subject was out in the open, I needed my Uncle Jack as well.

When they walked into my home, it was as if all was right with my life. I have no idea how long they stayed. It was several days, but probably not a week. They moved right on in.

They kept me company. They hung around with me. They blended into the family.

Uncle Jack fixed breakfast daily and earned the new name of "Uncle Flapjack" from my son Drew.

We celebrated Father's Day together.

Uncle Jack helped me with a project I was working on that involved piecing together our family tree. He gave me a wealth of information I had never had, including the little-known fact that my grandfather ran away to join a circus at the age of twelve. He was a snake charmer! And, he dated an armless woman!

How could anyone top that?

We spent hours reliving the endless trail of stories and memories that weave our lives together. They reminded me of the young boy I was to them as well as the man they still knew me to be.

They also brought me the one thing my friend, Chris, had told me I so desperately needed. A refresher course in letting others care for me.

That course was easy with Pam and Uncle Jack as my nursemaids. They were the perfect teachers because they had been there all along.

All I had to do was ask.

Lesson 17

Ask.

And you

just might

receive.

Chapter 18

Camp Songs

MY PARENTS NEVER sent me to camp. But then again, very few kids where I grew up went to a bona fide camp.

The closest I came to attending camp was the summer between my sophomore and junior years in high school. It was Camp Christian Day Camp, located a couple of miles outside my hometown. I was the one male out of a grand total of three camp counselors.

That I had no firsthand knowledge with camps, campers, or the camping experience was irrelevant. It sounded fun to me and I fig-ured—like with most things in my life—I could wing it.

The two female counselors embraced me into their circle instantly. Kelly was a year younger than me. She was cute, fun, and energetic.

Above: That's me with one of my favorite campers, Maggie.

Chris was four years older than me. She had worked at the camp the prior year so she was put in charge as the senior counselor. Chris and Kelly had a friendship in place before I came into the picture. They were more of a "big sister–little sister" kind of duo and their warm, playful relationship set the tone for the entire summer.

Our camp ran every day, Monday through Saturday morning, with a sleepover on Friday nights. We had a different group of kids each week.

The normal routine was to meet at our local YMCA at nine o'clock every morning. From there we would take a dirty yellow school bus out to the camp where we would spend the day—until mid-after-noon—keeping the kids busy with games, crafts, singing, swimming, and sports.

The camp was not fancy. In fact, it was kind of run down. Covering about fifteen acres, it had a small swimming lake and an abundance of mature trees that provided much-needed shade from the relentless Nebraska summer sun.

We had a main building with white wooden siding, green shingles, and a squeaky screened door. It had a primitive kitchen, a bathroom, and a bunch of picnic tables we would use for crafts and any other activity that needed to be done indoors.

Aside from a few eight-person cabins, with wooden floors and a lot of cobwebs, there wasn't much more to the camp.

Of course, there was a flagpole. It stood near the middle of a big open field. It was metal. Painted. In fact, you could tell it had been painted several times because you could see different colors of paint peeking out from behind all of the chips and nicks. It was at that flag-pole we began the program each day.

Our campers ranged in age from six to twelve years old. Some weeks we had fewer than ten kids. Other weeks we had twenty to thirty kids. As was the norm in my hometown, we had a broad mix of backgrounds. Some of the boys and girls were from low-income fami-lies while others came from families with second homes in Colorado.

Every weekend, Chris, Kelly, and I would plan out the schedule for the following week. There were many activities we'd repeat week after week. Swimming, fishing, archery, or nature hikes. But we also did a pretty good job integrating different crafts each week. New songs. New games. We even gave each week a "theme." Olympics. Cowboys. The campers liked that.

There were weeks we didn't want to end. Those were the weeks with cute, cooperative, spirited kids. With those kinds of campers, all the activities were fun. Nothing flopped.

There were other weeks, however, we wanted to end by mid-morning on Tuesday. Not only can one tough kid ruin the experience for all the other campers, he can also drain the energy out of the leaders.

I kept a journal that summer. While I wrote daily about the fun and featherbrained antics, I also chronicled what those experiences taught me about people through the wide, diverse spectrum of campers. I learned that all of the kids—regardless of their socioeconomic background, age, or gender—really wanted, and needed, the same things.

They needed reinforcement that they were capable of doing anything. They needed us to believe in them because, in return, it helped them believe in themselves. Some of the kids undoubtedly struggled in school. Some of them clearly had tough home lives. Camp was where they could be someone different. Camp was where they could experience success, if only for a few hours. Chris, Kelly, and I became their cheerleaders. And the kids fed on that.

I learned that all kids need to express themselves creatively. Be it through crafts, music, skits, or games, they need a safe environment in which to explore who they are. I was constantly amazed at situations where the toughest ten-year-old boy was also the one kid who didn't want to leave the craft table, or could pick up a guitar and lead the entire group in a song.

Finally, each and every child needed hugs. Sometimes, there simply weren't the right words to deal with a situation. But a good hug from one of the three of us usually did the trick. It gave the child whatever message was needed at the time. Someone cared. They weren't alone. Everything would be all right.

I loved being a camp counselor. I loved every experience of every day. But being at a camp made me wish I, too, could have had a real "go-to-summer-camp" experience.

And I often wondered what I missed by not having one.

―――――――――

BEING SICK, HAVING an illness, or recovering from surgery stinks. But, as odd as it sounds, it also makes you more approachable to the people who love you. To be perfectly blunt, it forces people to consider a world without you. And in many ways, that's not such a bad thing for all of us to consider in our relationships with the people we love.

I have three remarkable children. They are all loving. They are all funny. And they all have compassion in their hearts.

But let's be honest—they are still kids. And they act like kids sometimes.

They can say hurtful things. They slam doors. They think I'm the worst father on the face of the earth sometimes.

But my illness brought out a quality in each of my children that I had never seen before.

Perhaps it was just a quality within each of them I hadn't taken the time to notice. And enjoy.

My illness turned my three children—Kevin, Wallis, and Drew—into my camp counselors. For the entire summer.

The story starts with Drew, the youngest. Life before him was relatively calm.

At the time Drew was born, Kevin was an angelic-looking kindergartener and Wallis was an adorable preschooler. Perfectly dressed, always with a big bow in her hair.

From all perspectives, we were the picture-perfect family.

The idea of a third child was to mix things up—in a variety-is-the-spice-of-life way.

And, lo and behold, out popped Drew.

Truthfully, Drew surpassed everyone's wildest dreams. He had spirit. He had fire. He had electricity. He was the child who said from day one there was a lot of living to experience. A little wild? Sure. A challenge for teachers? Yup.

That's Drew.

During my summer at home, Drew went (much to my envy) to a *real* summer day camp. It was called Banner Day Camp. I called it magic. Every day Drew's bus would pick him up at 9:00 AM to take him away to another day of fun and adventure. And every afternoon, somewhere between 3:30 and 3:35 PM, his bus would bring him back home again.

I lived by that schedule. I waited every day for Drew's bus to bring him back to me.

And more than anything, I waited for the one thing I knew Drew would always bring me. His hug.

For all his roughness, his wildness, his craziness, and his out-of-control ways, Drew is the best hugger on the planet. There is no one like him.

At first, shortly after my surgery, Drew was guarded with his hugs. He knew I was sore. So he would hug my arm or he'd pull me down and snuggle with my head.

But as the weeks went by, he learned he could give me his trademark bear hug. That would be the one where he runs full speed at you. Where his eyes become a homing device. Where he hits you with all his weight. Where he buries his head in your stomach. Where he wraps his arms—fully extended—around your torso as he calls out your name.

And he doesn't let go.

I got one of those hugs every day. I got one on good days. I got one on bad days. It didn't matter to Drew.

And each one reminded me that everything was all right.

Wallis was thirteen when I had my surgery.

That would make her a 100 percent teenage girl. And that would make me the father of a 100 percent teenage girl. I'm told that's usually a recipe for disaster—with years of not communicating with each other.

But it didn't work that way for us.

You see, my thirteen-year-old daughter became something fantastically inspiring to me.

She became my cheerleader.

Wallis was certainly not a quiet child, but compared to her two brothers she is the one who has fewer words to share. She's more thoughtful in what she says. Sometimes she holds back a little. What I've learned through the years, however, is to really listen to her when she chooses to say something. Because her words always have meaning.

Early on, when I was first diagnosed, I wondered how Wallis would cope with my surgery. I wouldn't have blamed her if she had been embarrassed by it all.

But she never was. She simply cheered me on.

Without fail.

A week or so after I had all of my stitches removed and had been given the "OK" from my doctor to get into the pool, Wallis came out late one afternoon as I was trying so hard to swim. It was a very painful, difficult moment because it made me realize how much work I had in front of me.

I felt like an eighty-two-year-old man. I couldn't get my arms out of the water. At all. I couldn't kick because I thought my entire insides would split open. I couldn't stretch out my body. I felt permanently bent.

I had been swimming—kind of—for maybe two minutes. I was trying so hard, but I just couldn't do it. I was standing in the water.

That was when Wallis appeared.

She sat on the side of the pool with her legs dangling in the water.

"Hi Dad."

"Hey Wallis. How was your day?" I asked her as I proceeded to slowly move across the water.

She started to tell me about her day. The small details of her last few hours.

"Does it feel good to be back in the water?"

"Sure, but I'm embarrassed to have you see me like this."

That's when she said three words I will never forget. Three words that—from my perspective as a forty-four-year-old dad of this beautiful young girl—gave me strength, hope, and determination.

"Dad, you're *awesome*!"

Then she proceeded to tell me all of the reasons *why* she thought I was awesome.

By that point, I had stopped swimming and was standing in the pool next to her. I placed my arms on the side of the pool and rested my head on my forearms as I listened to my daughter give me my daily dose of cheerleading.

Awesome.

My daughter told me I was awesome.

And upon hearing her words, that's precisely how I felt.

Kevin.

The oldest.

Everyone should have Kevin as their oldest child. He has the job down pat.

I was the youngest. I had different pressures. But I certainly had none of the pressures of being the oldest. I had four older brothers who paved the way for me. I had four older brothers who wore my parents down.

I simply got to reap the benefits.

But this isn't a story about what a good job Kevin does at being the oldest child. This isn't a story about how much pressure Kevin deals with as I try out new parenting techniques on him. This isn't a story about the countless good examples Kevin sets for his younger siblings or the good decisions he has always made in his life.

This is a story about Kevin and his music.

It's funny. I remember the summer when Kevin was thirteen. I had signed him up for a short introductory guitar class. He was furious with me for forcing him to go.

I remember almost giving in and letting him skip out of it.

I also remember the fire in his eyes after his first lesson. He was hooked. His life would never be the same.

Nor would mine. Thankfully.

Kevin became the musician in the family. He learned how to express his feelings and emotions through music. When he was happy, he turned to his music. When he was troubled, his music was his release.

His music became an extension of him.

And he became my camp counselor who would always pull out his guitar when I most needed it.

From my usual resting spot outside, I had the best seat in the house as I watched the ongoing procession of people I loved stroll outside to take their place next to me.

And Kevin was always one of my favorite acts.

Wearing nothing but his colorful bathing suit and a very large black cowboy hat, Kevin regularly made his way outside to sit with me.

"Hey Dad, what's up?"

"Not much. You?"

"I'm learning a new song. You wanna hear it? But I'm warning you, it's not very good."

"Absolutely!" I'd always reply.

And I meant it.

Then my camp counselor would serenade me. Sometimes for four minutes. Sometimes for forty. We spoke very little. I just listened.

I was no longer taking medication for the pain. I didn't need it. Kevin's music was my medicine.

And I was addicted to it.

Thirty years. That's about how long it had been since I was a summer camp counselor.

Thirty years. That's how long it had been since I played that role to all of those terrific little kids who were going through their journey in life.

And here I was.

Having my first summer camp experience.

And I had the three best counselors ever.

Lesson 18

There's
a camper—and
a counselor—
inside us all.

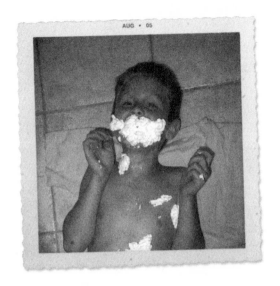

Chapter 19

Whipped Cream Wonders

MY BROTHER MICK invented the game.

It was something we played only during the summer. We played it at our cabin. It was a game we'd enjoy once the sun had set, while our parents sat outside on the patio with a nightcap—enjoying the sound of crickets and the gentle flow of waves made by a passing pontoon boat.

It was a game played only by the children—much to the disgust of the mothers.

The game involved slingshots. And toads.

At nighttime, our beach became infested with literally hundreds of toads. They were attracted to the area by the three floodlights that

Above: Drew demonstrating the famous whipped cream trick!

were attached to the eves of the simple, one-story cabin. As little kids, we would find great joy in catching the toads with our hands, and placing them in a small, plastic, rectangular bucket of water that always sat at the edge of our patio. It was the "dip" bucket, the bucket you'd step into as you transitioned from the beach to the patio—to rinse off all of the sand that was stuck to your feet.

But at night, the "dip" bucket became the toad jail.

Depending on the size of the toads—and they did have an enormous range in plumpness and girth—we could probably put anywhere from ten to thirty toads in the dip bucket.

Our goal was to trick one of the mothers to unknowingly step into the dip bucket full of toads. Just thinking about it made us giddy. I'm not sure if a mom ever fell for the trick, but it was certainly fun preparing for it.

Somewhere along the line, however, Mick came up with a different idea. And that's where his game was invented.

It started innocently.

Really.

Family friends were visiting, and we had finished dinner, which consisted of hamburgers and hotdogs on the Weber grill, corn on the cob, coleslaw, and Jell-O. That was our routine dinner when we had company. As dusk was setting in, and the parents were cleaning up in the kitchen, I grabbed the two little kids and told them to join me in our evening tradition of catching toads. Hesitant at first, they quickly realized that the act of catching toads was fun, and they squealed in delight as they began to help place toad after toad in the rectangular dip bucket.

Enter Mick.

He and my brother Kevin were down at the lake, standing on the sandy part of the beach that stayed wet from the steady sway of waves made by the passing boats. They had slingshots and a mound of balls made from the wet sand below their feet. One by one, they would take turns shooting the "sand balls" and laugh as each one exploded into millions of pieces of sand.

That's when it happened. That's when the new game was invented.

"You guys want to see something cool?" Mick asked us.

"Sure!" we all replied.

"Bring the dip bucket down here," he said, wearing a grin on his face as he whispered something to Kevin.

There we all stood: our two visiting friends, Kevin, Mick, and me. A couple of slingshots. A bucket of toads. And the water before us.

Mick bent down and grabbed a toad as we all watched. He placed the plump thing in the middle of his slingshot—between the prongs— and in a split second sent the little guy on a first-class transatlantic trip!

After the shock of what we had just witnessed, and when we could see the toad start to swim back to us, we all giggled and tried our turns at the new game.

Toad slingshotting was born, and we played it every summer with numerous unsuspecting guests.

Our cabin was home to countless parties, a revolving door of gatherings. It was a place to connect with family, friends, and people to whom my parents wanted to extend the reach of their embracing arms.

Sometimes it would be one family. Sometimes it would be multiple families. Sometimes it would be an older couple who lived down the street. Or it might be our priests. It might have been a sleepover where I invited a friend or two to spend the night. Perhaps the guest was a widow whose bare feet hadn't touched sand in over thirty years. Or it could have been a party just for the teenagers—with lots of food, music, and fun.

But there was almost always some kind of a celebration in the works at our cabin. My parents could turn anything into a celebration. They believed in the importance of sharing with others. They made a conscious effort to do so.

Most of the time, that effort only involved picking up the phone and calling someone.

Celebrating is really quite simple.

———————————

WHEN KEVIN, WALLIS, AND DREW were younger, I used to have a "trick" I'd do for them when they had friends over to the house.

It was called the "whipped cream" trick.

And like most tricks all good dads do, there really was no trick involved. It was nothing more than pure silliness.

The trick involved a can of aerosol whipped cream. Every family with kids has one. It's a metal canister with a long-necked plastic cap. It looks like a spaceship. And it has a flexible plastic nozzle. After you shake it up, you can squirt out the most fantastically frothy-luscious cream. We always seemed to have at least one can hanging out in our refrigerator.

The trick involved having the child lie on the ground as I dropped little bits of the whipped cream from the can into their mouth.

First from about six inches away. Then twelve inches.

Then more.

And, of course, the higher the can rose above the children's heads, the more likely the dollops of whipped cream were to land on their chins.

Or on their noses.

Or in their eyes.

All the while the child would laugh uncontrollably. As would all those who witnessed the trick.

Inevitably, everyone in attendance would beg to have a chance to participate.

Our family has a long-standing reputation as fun, creative entertainers.

We have put together some pretty memorable parties over the years for friends. Croquet tournaments. Cookie decorating "Olympics" at Christmastime. We could come up with a fun theme for any occasion. The same standards of creativeness applied to our celebrations for Christmas, Easter, birthday parties, and even the team baseball party. They became a trademark in the Higley House.

Over the years, I actually became a blend of Martha and MacGyver. With enough newspaper and tempera paint, I could make the back deck look like a circus tent or the sunroom look like a pirate ship. While I'm confident everyone in attendance had fun, these parties were exhausting to put together, and the cleanup wasn't much fun either.

But cancer, surgery, and recovery helped bring a wrecking ball to any form of over-the-top entertaining that summer. However, there was always a steady flow of people coming and going out of the house. And everyone always appeared to be having a darn good time.

Which brings me to one of the favorite things I learned that summer. I learned the difference between entertaining and celebrating. Entertaining can be a lot of work. Celebrating, on the other hand, needs only one other person and some good attitudes. The rest just happens.

Thanks to Drew, a fair number of those celebrations that summer included the untapped potential in that can of aerosol whipped cream. It had been patiently waiting in the refrigerator for us behind the pulp-free orange juice and the spare gallon of 1 percent milk.

Drew was a master at setting the stage for friends of all ages.

"Hey Dad, you should do the whipped cream trick tonight!"

It was a line that always got a response from our guests.

"What's the whipped cream trick?" they would ask. So easily would they walk into our trap.

"No, no, no," I would reply. "It's too late. Really."

"Come on, Dad. Please!" Drew would plead.

As with dangling a nice big juicy worm in front of the mouth of a fish, our guests were about to be hooked.

"OK. OK. But I'm going to need a volunteer to help."

And I would always get a guest to volunteer.

The evening usually would include most everyone taking a turn, lying on the floor and getting covered with whipped cream. Yes, it was a mess.

But we had something to celebrate.

Lesson 19

Celebrate

something

every day.

Chapter 20

I'd Rather Be the Jackson Five

ON THE FIRST day of kindergarten, my teacher, Mrs. Newkirk, walked around the classroom and gave each of us fresh-faced five-year-olds a sheet of paper with a mimeographed image of a storybook house—complete with swirly smoke coming out of the chimney—and the words "My Family" written across the top. The rest of the sheet was blank.

"Put this in your folder and take it home with you today," she told us. "Your homework for tonight is to show me what your family looks like. You can draw them or you can even use real photographs if your mom and dad help you!"

Above: On the bottom are Dave (left) and Tom. Kevin's on top of Dave. Mick's next to Kevin. And that's me on top—for the moment.

I was so excited to have homework. My first homework! And I wasn't about to ask for any help from anyone.

My finished product was made with cutout pictures showing my family. There was a mom, a dad, four big brothers, and me. It was a model family. Literally.

I had cut every picture out of the JCPenney catalog. The mom and dad were much younger than my actual parents. The dad had a full head of hair and the mom had on a spotlessly clean dress, gloves, and pearls. To make my twin brothers, I took two pictures of the same boy—one time wearing a raincoat and the other time wearing pajamas. I was sure it would pass for my twin brothers. For my other two brothers, I included a picture of two boys dressed in football jerseys and sporting big, friendly smiles. And then there was me, or at least the image of me—an extremely cute little boy wearing shorts and a collared shirt.

And that was my fantasy family.

Perhaps I should have been in therapy back then.

I went through most of my childhood feeling like my brothers didn't like me. I felt it the most when my parents were gone on a Friday or a Saturday night, leaving me alone with my brothers. That was not a good thing. Not good at all.

Mick and Kevin (also known as the two football players in my family montage) were pros at playing with my head.

One particular Saturday night, our parents were away playing bridge with another couple, and Mick and Kevin were put in charge of a six-year-old me.

I don't remember the specifics of the night. But I do remember fighting with them. Both of them. I remember arguing nonstop. I remember being outraged. And I remember taking a small ukulele my parents bought in Mexico and smashing it over Kevin's head.

Then I remember running and hiding in a closet.

Which was followed by several minutes of silence.

Next, I remember hearing my eleven-year-old brother, Mick, screaming, "Oh my God! Oh my God! Someone help me! Oh my God! Someone call Mom and Dad! Oh my God!"

I ran out of the closet. My heart was pounding.

I found Mick. He was in the kitchen, standing over Kevin's lifeless body slumped on the floor. Kevin's head was covered in . . . blood!

"He's dead!" Mick screamed. "He's dead!"

And before I could break out in the tears that were building up inside of me, knowing I was going to be in *big* trouble with my parents for killing my brother, Kevin rose miraculously!

Suddenly, Mick pinned me from behind while Kevin beat the crap out of me.

His blood? Catsup.

His death? Faked.

His motivation? Obvious. I was the one who was going to be killed that night.

I gave my brothers a multitude of reasons not to like me as a little kid. I was, after all, a pain-in-the-neck most of the time.

I hated being the baby. I asked my mother one day if we might ever have another kid. It seemed like a reasonable request to me. I don't remember her exact response, but I do remember my question really set her off and whatever she said ended with the words "Are you out of your mind?"

My role was carved in stone from the day I was born. Boy number five. The baby brother.

And that, much to my regret, was who I had to be.

BRINGING MY BROTHERS—Tom, Dave, and Mick—into my cancer story was one of the hardest things I had to do. As a family, we had been down the cancer road three other times together. Two of those times had taken place in the previous six years. The wounds were too raw. There was also a part of me that felt as if I was letting them down. Cancer can make you think stupid sometimes.

As I prepared myself to call each of my three brothers, I relived the pain I had felt a few years earlier when my brother Mick called to tell me Kevin had brain cancer. I couldn't bear to start my brothers on another emotional roller coaster.

My love for my brothers is a love reserved solely for them. Through the last twenty-some years of adulthood, we've had to adjust our relationships to fit into our grown-up lives. There was a point in time when we lived in five very distant states: California, New York, North Carolina, Kansas, and Nebraska. Our careers were demanding. Our own families consumed our time.

And while we always stayed in touch, our connections became more structured and formal. We'd focus on rendezvousing back in Nebraska. We'd visit each other on occasion. But we were always on a schedule. And we had little downtime.

Some people joke that as they get older, they only see their relatives at funerals. My brothers and I were getting into that groove at a very early age.

My cancer story, in the scheme of the Higley family, was the first one that didn't come with an automatic death sentence. There was a small part of me that even felt like I had a purpose, a duty of sorts, in being the first one in our family to survive this. It was the hope of vindication perhaps.

Maybe I just wanted my brothers to be proud of me.

Every day of that summer I wrote in the notebook my friend Karen had given me.

But I rarely found myself writing about what was going on with my cancer storyline.

The stories that kept bubbling up to my head, through my heart, were stories from the past. Things I hadn't thought about in years. And so many of them were about my brothers. The real stories of who they were and continued to be to me.

- Sitting next to each other, in birth order, at our kitchen counter eating our morning bowls of cereal.
- Building a human pyramid in our backyard. My dad always placing me on top.
- Idolizing my brother Kevin as I sat on a stool in his darkroom. Watching him develop black-and-white photographs.
- Counting free throw shots for Mick. Wishing I was him.
- Waxing the car with the twins before they went to their one and only prom.
- Flipping off Mick from afar and thinking I was pretty cool. And having him, several hours later, give me a much-needed lesson in respect.

I wrote about the endless collection of stories that shaped my life. I wrote about my family.

I had four amazing brothers growing up. And now I had three.

That summer, the three of them gave me something that could only come from them. It was the reminder of something I had forgotten I loved so much.

Being their little brother.

Lesson 20

Embrace

who

you are.

Chapter 21

But I Want a Puppy!

MY FIFTH BIRTHDAY was outstanding.

For starters, my parents had a party for me—my first—and invited all the neighborhood kids. At the drugstore we bought invitations that had cowboys and horses on them, and I watched with jubilation and anticipation as my mom wrote down the details of the party on the preprinted lines on the inside of the cards. The best part was seeing my name, handwritten by my mom, so it read:

"It's a Birthday Party for *Jimmy*!"

I was turning five. I was about to start kindergarten. And my time had arrived.

Above: My fifth birthday party. The gold standard for all future birthdays.

To further add to my excitement, my mom took me to our local department store to buy me new clothes to wear to the party!

New clothes! I hardly ever got new clothes!

And I was sure I looked just like the boys in the Sears catalog once I put on my new red shorts and seersucker shirt.

During the week before the party, I planned games and activities with my mom. We went shopping for prizes. We ordered a cake at the Vienna Bakery. It was going to have my name on it. MINE!

I was on "center-of-attention" overload. (Adding to the list of reasons my brothers didn't like me.)

So, enjoying the spotlight I rarely had, I decided to do what any almost-five-year-old would do. I asked for a puppy as my birthday present.

I figured, "Why not?" We used to have a dog. From my self-centered point of view, it seemed like the perfect time for my parents to give me a puppy.

My mom ignored my request. I decided she was acting. But I knew she had something planned. I knew there would be a puppy in this story!

The day of my party was a warm, sunny, perfect August day. I woke up at the crack of dawn and immediately put on my new clothes four hours before the party began.

My mom was up and had already set our family table for the party. It had a white plastic tablecloth on it (we never had tablecloths!) with cups and plates that had the same cowboy and horses that adorned my invitations. The cake in the middle of the table was round and said "Happy Birthday Jimmy," which was very cool. What *wasn't* cool was all of the big frilly flowers on the top of the cake. Flowers? This was a cowboy party. Where were the horses?

But that aside, the BEST part of the table was that my mom covered it with M&Ms. Everywhere. Hundreds if not millions of M&Ms were spread out all over the table. And she said we could eat ALL of them at the party.

Five-year-old heaven.

My friends arrived at eleven o'clock, and we proceeded to play all of the backyard games my mom and I had planned. My brother Mick even helped out. And he was nice!

My mom had us come inside to eat and open gifts. I don't recall what we actually had to eat, because as soon as I sat down, I spilled an entire paper cup of red Kool-Aid all over the table and myself—soaking my clothes to the skin. And ruining a couple of hundred M&Ms.

So, I had to make an unplanned departure from my own party and put on a pair of torn, old blue jeans and a T-shirt. I was longer to be mistaken for one of the boys in the Sears catalog.

But I did get a lot of gifts, so I quickly forgot my table disaster. My buddy Kirk gave me a cash register that looked just like a real one in the stores. And Kristin gave me a gun set I was sure would be good for using on my brothers.

And, while all of us were enjoying the sugar high from too much cake and the salvaged M&Ms, I was perfectly aware there was still one more gift awaiting me somewhere in the house.

A puppy. My puppy.

Would I get it when all of my friends were there?

Would I get it later that day when my dad got home from work?

Or would it be hidden up in my bedroom in one of those big boxes with holes cut in the sides so I could take it to bed with me and hug it all night?

Of course, in the end, there was no puppy.

There was the party with the cool invitations.

There were the fun games with a brother who even helped.

There were new clothes.

A cake with roses (yuck) and my name on it.

There were M&Ms.

And there were gifts galore.

It was a great birthday. But I was still kind of sad.

Because there was no puppy.

Fast-forward one year: The puppy arrived the day before my sixth birthday. I had long stopped asking for one. But that summer day one year later, my parents piled all five of us into the car and drove to Omaha to pick out a puppy at a small, rundown pet store.

We chose a ten-week-old mutt and named her Trixie.

She arrived in our family on that uneventful August day. And she enjoyed the enviable role of "Super Dog" in our house for thirteen long years.

IT WAS AUGUST, my birthday month. Almost three months after surgery. By all accounts, it should have been the best birthday of my life.

I was nearing the end of a summer of healing. My doctor gave me the green light to go back to work whenever I wanted to. The truth was I didn't want to.

My cancer remained an unresolved issue, and I was learning to live life with a new regime of daily medications to keep the dormant cancer cells I likely still had in my body at bay.

"We'll keep watching for it, and we'll check you every three months so we can be on top of it when it comes back," my doctor told me.

Grateful? Of course. Frustrated? Yup.

But I was equally frustrated that the issue of my "gift" was also unresolved. I never found it. This extraordinary thing Karen promised hadn't arrived. I looked so hard I practically willed it to happen. So, while I had an amazing summer of reflection, nothing—my health or my gift—ended the way I had originally dreamed.

There were so many things I had cherished over the three months of recuperating. Let me rephrase that. I *cherished* my three months of recuperating. I felt alive every day and I was afraid to go back to a world where that feeling would stop.

And now it was time to look at my calendar to figure out a day to resume work.

My time was running out.

I wondered if maybe I actually did find the gift but just hadn't figured it out. I could certainly *tell* people about all the things I had experienced that summer. I had learned the importance of slowing down and celebrating the people in my life, and the importance of being more honest and loving with people. I could say I had learned to see my children's gifts or I needed to look hard at my professional career and do some serious soul searching regarding my commitment to it. I could say all of that. And it would be true.

But what wouldn't be true would be to say I had that super-amazing "Aha!" moment.

And I was coming to terms with the likelihood of being disappointed. Quietly and silently.

Lesson 21

The

best gifts

find you.

Let it happen.

Chapter 22

I Hate You, Donny Osmond

WITH FOUR OLDER brothers, I rarely received any new clothes. My closet was full of hand-me-downs. Actually, because two of those brothers were twins, I often had duplicates of everything.

Two blue blazers.

Two pairs of penny loafers.

Two bathrobes.

Bottom line, I was never short of clothes.

Once a year, however, my mom would treat me to a few new things. That would be in August, before school started.

We called it, appropriately enough, "school shopping."

And I loved it.

Above: My first day of kindergarten and my initial attempt at making a fashion statement.

Our options for clothes shopping were pretty limited in my small Nebraska hometown. We did have a JCPenney store, though, and that was where my parents tended to buy most of my clothes. Every so often, however, my mom would splurge and drive thirty minutes to Omaha where our purchasing options were much better.

I remember wondering, year after year, if I had grown enough to wear bigger clothes. I progressed nicely through the routine boy sizes—eight, ten, twelve—until the year my mom told me she thought we should try a "husky" boy size.

Husky? I thought. *Is she telling me I'm fat*?

None of my brothers was overweight. Not a bit. So my biggest fear was the four of them finding out about my new "husky" size.

They did.

And, of course, they humiliated me.

Suddenly, school shopping wasn't fun anymore.

Fortunately, that phase lasted only one year. By the following August, I was back to "regular" sizes, and I was hoping to find some "Donny Osmond" looking clothes—bell-bottoms, shirts with big, puffy sleeves, vests, and platform shoes.

We scored—HUGE—at the Sears department store in Omaha. I was, without a doubt, going to be the coolest looking twelve-year-old boy in my entire ZIP code.

And I couldn't wait to go back to school.

I DID NOT want to go back to work. Not. Not. Not. That feeling was very apparent to me as I stood staring into my closet, reacquainting myself with my work wardrobe a few days before my scheduled return.

I couldn't remember the last time I had worn long pants. For three months, my idea of "dressing up" meant putting on the only pair of shorts I owned that didn't have holes.

So I decided a few additions to my wardrobe might make me feel better. New clothes. New attitude. That always used to work when I was a kid.

Shopping, in general, isn't my thing. Mall shopping, in particular, is definitely not my thing.

As I stood in the men's dressing room in my boxer shorts debating over the 31-inch-long khakis or the 32-inch version, I knew the world I was about to step back into probably wasn't my thing either.

For some reason, new clothes weren't having the same impact they did when I was a kid.

And I still didn't look anything like Donny Osmond.

Lesson 22

Life is a series

of transitions.

Eventually,

you need to

move on.

Chapter 23

Dear Glady ...

MY MOM'S CLOSEST friend was Glady. They met at church when they were both thirteen years old, became instant best friends, and remained so until the day my mom died.

Their lives took them in different directions after high school. My mom worked for a few years, went to college, met and married my dad, and spent her life in Nebraska raising my brothers and me.

Glady, on the other hand, met her husband, Dap, a couple of years out of high school while working in Oak Ridge, Tennessee. They wed

---

Above: That's Glady on the right. My mom's favorite person on earth.

when Glady was in her early twenties and spent a lifetime living in and traveling to interesting and exotic places around the world.

But Glady and my mom were always connected. They maintained their relationship through a never-ending exchange of letters.

Letters that they mailed.

Letters with stamps.

Letters filled with stories about their lives.

My mom and Glady both wrote the most vivid, detailed, and funny letters.

Their letters were typewritten. Mom typed hers on a Smith-Corona typewriter she had acquired when she was in college. She expressed her thoughts through that typewriter every day of her life.

In fact, she was typing a letter the night she got sick, days before she died.

I still have that half-written letter.

My mom kept her typewriter on a desk that was tucked away in a corner of my dad's den. Dad had a big, impressive rolltop desk that had been used by a judge. Conversely, Mom's desk was small, and it had numerous drawers. Every inch of that desk was used.

In the middle of the desk—center stage—was her typewriter.

And there was always a white piece of typing paper in it. A work-in-progress letter. Usually it was a letter to Glady, but Mom had several other friends and relatives she would write to, as well.

She rarely sat down and wrote a letter from beginning to end. Rather, she would start a letter, stop to run errands or work in the kitchen, and return to it when she could to add a few more paragraphs. Her letters were simply a part of her day.

They were a part of her.

When I was a grade-schooler, I'd sneak into my dad's den when my mom was in the kitchen and my dad was at work. I'd read her in-progress letters.

At the time, I never thought of it as inappropriate to be reading her letters. It was one more dimension in the process of understanding who my mom was.

And what was going on in her mind.

Her letters were usually several pages long. When they took more than one day to write, she would type the new date in the left-hand margin to let the reader know the words that followed were written on a new day.

I came to recognize three distinct things about my mom's letters.

For starters, they were about the day-to-day events of her life. She could write two paragraphs about the plumber who had been working in the house the day before and was going through personal problems—elaborating about their conversation, why she liked the guy, and how much the total bill was.

She could go into great detail about a new recipe she tried. She could give all of the specifics about my brothers' sporting events including how they performed and what she wore as she sat in the stands cheering them on. She could describe home improvement projects, sometimes sending small samples of fabric or carpet along with the letter to help give a better visual to the reader. She could describe what was blooming in her garden or how many hours she spent pulling weeds. She could talk about what her boys were doing that very moment. She could then proceed to talk about how many loads of dark-colored clothes she was able to push through the pipeline, a new song she heard on the radio, something different she was doing with her hair, or what happened with the dog at the vet that day.

She described the day-to-day events in her life because those were the things that were most important to her.

The second thing I remember about my mom's letters was the emotion she was able to share. She could move from factual information to vividly describing her feelings. And her emotions covered the range from absolute silliness to over-the-top tears of either sadness or joy. She could describe the pride she felt in witnessing one of her five sons' accomplishments, and she could fully explain the hurt she felt when a child said something rude to her when she was volunteering at school. Her letters were a wonderful blend of facts and feelings as she took the reader on a mini-journey of her world.

She expressed herself beautifully, sincerely, and intimately.

The third thing I remember about my mom's letters was her use of the "strike-through" key.

The strike-through key sits directly to the right of the number "0" on her old Smith-Corona typewriter's keyboard. It is a short, horizontal line that looks like this:

Back when my mom used a typewriter, she had two choices for making corrections. One option was to use an eraser to try to remove the undesired word. While this worked, it often resulted in a big smudge or, worse yet, a hole in the paper. The other option was to use the strike-through over the undesired words.

My mom used the second option. A lot. But it wasn't that she used it to correct misspelled words. She was a wonderful speller. She used it primarily when she wanted to change the way she expressed something. Perhaps her original words were a little too strong. Or maybe not strong enough. Or maybe once she wrote something down—and then read it—she realized she didn't exactly feel that way.

So she'd backspace, strike through the words or sentences she wanted to replace, and then type her new thoughts.

~~Leaving everything there for the reader to see. Every thought. Even those that changed. She was happy to reveal herself completely.~~

~~My mom was far from perfect. What she was, however, was real. Authentic. And extremely content with who and where she was.~~

Perfection was never a priority for her.

Finding joy in the moment, however, was.

I WENT BACK to work on a full-time basis the day after Labor Day. A new season had begun.

Stepping back into my business world made me feel somewhat like Dorothy when she woke up back in Kansas after her kaleidoscopic trip to Oz.

But I knew I wasn't waking up from a dream. In fact, I realized I had been more awake during the prior three months than I had been in years.

My second day back at work was a typical Wednesday morning. I was walking from the train station in downtown Chicago to my office. As I was walking along the bustling canyons of the financial district, I was thinking, as I usually do, about a number of things. This particular morning, I had two completely different thoughts rattling around in my head.

First, I was thinking about how I couldn't wait for it to be Friday. I wanted the next few days to pass so I could retreat—if only for a couple of days—to the world I had grown to love over the summer. The feeling I had—of not being content in the moment—was over-whelmingly unsettling.

The second thing I was thinking about was my mom. Specifically, I was thinking about her letter writing and how she freely put her thoughts out there. I smiled as I thought about her use of the strike-through key. A few weeks earlier I had stumbled upon the letter she was writing the night she became sick. It was a letter to my Aunt Bev and focused on my recent appendectomy. It included details about my 1:30 PM doctor's appointment, the decision to operate, the hooking up of my IV at 3:30 PM, and then . . . well, her letter stopped because the nightmare, the ambulance, the entire ordeal leading to her death, began.

And it was left unfinished.

Standing there in downtown Chicago, those two random thoughts morphed together and became one crystal clear message to me.

Why was I so anxious for it to be Friday? Wednesday wasn't even half over and I was already glossing over the next few days. More importantly, why was it bothering me so much that I wasn't happy being a part of the Wednesday world I was in?

Answers and clarity started to come to me as I began to understand what it was that I had loved and valued about the previous few months.

I had lived in the present all summer long. I absorbed what each moment brought.

And I only came to understand that when I caught myself—there on the second day back to work—realizing I was already falling into the trap of wanting it to be "a few days later." I wanted to be somewhere other than where I was at that time.

I hadn't even been back at the office a week and I was already resorting to my "old" way of thinking.

I stood there amid the swirl of morning rush hour synchronization in a frantic downtown Chicago, and I realized that every morning during my summer at home, I woke up happy. Excited to see what the day would bring to me.

And I never wanted a day to end.

As I continued my walk to the office, slipping in between the steady stampede of faceless workers, amid the honking cars, the police whistles, and the muffled sounds of commuters on their cell phones, I felt my mother's spirit. Not memories of her. It was her spirit. The joyful way she embraced every minute of her day. The good. The loud. The painful. The routine.

Living in the moment.

I had a summer experiencing life the way my mom had lived every day.

Was the gift Karen promised me as simple as that?

Lesson 23

~~Don't strive~~

~~for perfection.~~

Be authentic.

Be content.

Chapter 24

Snoopin' in Mom's Purse

THE WEEK FOLLOWING my mom's funeral, after my brothers had gone back to either college or their jobs, my dad and I were left alone to deal with the realities of being in a home that had no pulse.

After my first day back at school, I came home and found my dad standing motionless over a basket of dirty clothes. They were my mom's dirty clothes. They were the clothes she had worn a day or two before she got sick. And like everything in our home now, they were lifeless.

"We need to go through her stuff," my dad said to me.

Above: I like this picture of my mom on her last birthday. Hey, check out those huge mums in front of our house!

"I know," I replied.

What I really wanted to do was lash back at him and ask how in the world could he get rid of Mom's things. But I soon found myself playing the loyal assistant as we methodically sorted through the world she left behind.

We cleaned out her closet and dresser. I remembered when she had worn each and every item. A red pleated dress she reserved for the holidays. The ugly pink robe—complete with a matching nightgown—my dad had given her on their last anniversary. Countless blouses that were part of her daily mom uniform. There were a few things we saved. A skirt that she never actually wore but was determined to fit into one day. A shawl that often doubled as a tablecloth. An embroidered skirt she had bought in Mexico. She loved these things. And they weren't leaving the house. Not yet.

We went through her jewelry, which was mostly costume. She had a charm bracelet that had belonged to her mother, Lillian. We kept that. I found my mom's engagement ring—her only nice piece of jewelry—in an envelope with the hospital's name on it. We placed that aside with the charm bracelet.

We cleaned out the drawers in the bathroom where she kept her toiletries. Her toothbrush. A hairbrush with strands of her hair in it. Some makeup cases I don't think she ever used. The only thing we didn't toss was her one bottle of perfume. I never really liked it when my mom wore perfume. She called it "foo-foo-juice." I called it stinky. But now I wanted to inhale that stinky smell. A quick spray of it in the air, and when I closed my eyes, she'd actually come back—for a moment.

We cleaned out her desk. I read over her calendar and ached at all of the appointments she had in the coming weeks. She needed to be here. I needed her to be here.

We took her coats out of the front closet. Her white raincoat with oversized black buttons. A red windbreaker. Her favorite, a suede coat with sheepskin lining that was reserved for winter. They all had a pair of gloves in the pockets. And a white linen hanky. But now they were simply heaped on the growing pile destined for a local charity.

Finally, we cleaned out her purse. Her unfinished pack of Dentyne gum—with one small stick remaining—went into the trash. My dad took her credit cards and driver's license. We saved her favorite linen hanky.

Inside her wallet I found something I never knew she carried. It was a piece of white paper—about the size of a credit card—with something typed on it. My mom had typed it.

I shall pass through
this world but once.

If, therefore, there
be any kindness I can show,

Or good thing
I can do,

let me do it now.

Let me not defer it.
For I shall not pass
this way again.

—Stephen Grellet
(1773–1855)

I recognized those words from a birthday card someone had once given my mom. That card sat on her desk for years. It obviously meant something to her.

I knew I was intended to find that dog-eared message. My mom must have left it for me. Be kind. Every day. Be kind. Just like Mom.

So I took that piece of paper and tucked it inside my own wallet. It stayed there for years. I always knew where it was. Then, somewhere along the course of my life, it ultimately found a more permanent home inside a small frame.

And from that day forward, it stood on the desk in my den.

DID I FIND my gift that Wednesday morning while I was walking to work? Was Karen's promised gift simply the reminder that I needed to live in the moment? That seemed trite. Anticlimactic. There had to be more. I wanted something I could get my arms around!

All through that day, the dots of my life experiences kept coming back to me. I could see them. I kept thinking to myself this must be what people talk about when their lives flash before their eyes. Except, I wasn't dying. But I felt as if memories from my life were hitting me from every direction. Big things. Little things. Insignificant things.

I had thought about many of them over the last three months. But they continued to present themselves to me that day—all at lightning speed. I knew there was something more to this than the simple message of "live in the moment." I needed to understand, however, why all these images from my past continued to race in my head.

One thing kept playing over and over like a needle skipping on an old record. It was the piece of paper I had found in my mom's wallet many years ago. There was something about it that was hanging heavy with me. Could it possibly tie in to any of this? Sure, the poem was about showing kindness to others. That fit and tied into the importance of living in the moment.

Maybe the message on that piece of paper was the *real* gift?

I played this out in my head all day long. I was sure there was more and couldn't wait to get home and read those words in the picture frame on my desk. I hadn't looked at them in years. Maybe I would see something different today?

As soon as I arrived home, I ran into my den and grabbed the frame. I read the words of the French Quaker missionary, though I had memorized them long before.

I shall pass through
this world but once.

If, therefore, there
be any kindness I can show,

Or good thing
I can do,

let me do it now.

Let me not defer it.
For I shall not pass
this way again.

—Stephen Grellet
(1773–1855)

Yes, the poem was exactly as I had remembered it. *Then it hit me.* How could I have forgotten? There *was* something else. My mom had also typed something on the flip side of the paper!

I opened up the frame and carefully dismantled the cardboard so I could get to the worn piece of paper. I had chills as I took the backing off the frame to reveal the old, familiar piece of paper.

Then I saw it. The second message on the back.

> This is the beginning of a new day. God has given me this day to use as I will. I can waste it—or use it for good, but what I do today is important, because I am exchanging a day of my life for it! When tomorrow comes, this day will be gone forever, leaving in its place something that I have traded for it. I want it to be gain, and not loss; good, and not evil; success, and not failure; in order that I shall not regret the price that I have paid for it.
>
> —Heartsill Wilson

I had last seen those words more than thirty years earlier. More specifically, I had "exchanged" more than ten thousand "todays" since I had last read them.

Finally, I understood my life-changing gift.

Most of our daily experiences come and go. They never register with us as anything more than the mundane events of our lives. But they are anything but mundane! Or meaningless!

Many of the things that have shaped and influenced my life have come from simple and seemingly insignificant moments. However, they ultimately became the experiences from which I would harvest the lessons in later years to help me make decisions. Find my path. Or give me strength.

Reading those words hidden on the back of the paper made me realize they were the words my mother lived by. Her cherished words helped me understand that every story in every today has the potential to be a lesson. If you miss a "today," you miss all of its lessons. That's *why* it's important to live in the moment.

My mom knew it. And I'm quite certain she rarely regretted the price she paid for any of her "todays"—too few as they were.

As I read the reverse side of that piece of paper again, I knew that Karen's promise had finally come true. I had received my life-changing gift. I also was holding the gift my mom left to me when I was fourteen years old. Best of all, I came to the realization that both gifts had always been there.

Every day of my life.

Lesson 24

Expect

the

unexpected.

Chapter 25

Wait, There's More!

HELEN KELLER ONCE said, "Life is a succession of lessons which must be lived to be understood."

What I came to understand that summer of healing is that lessons knock on our door every day. And many of those lessons can be found in the most unexpected places. So, if you're not tuning into your days you're likely going to miss a lesson.

Simple, right?

Actually, I think it's a simple concept that is hard to execute.

I had a lot of time on my hands that summer. I spent much of it reflecting on every aspect of my life. Each day, I found myself

Above: My mom. And her Smith-Corona. Working on a college paper. I still have that typewriter. One of my many reminders of Mom.

reconnecting with long-lost memories, and time after time I had proverbial moments where lightbulbs would flash on and exclamation points would dance over my head as I began to understand the experiences that shaped and influenced my life. In essence, I rediscovered my own life's lessons.

I also came to understand six things.

1. The experiences of my life have given me an abundance of lessons, which I draw from daily.

2. I've tucked away the memories of those lessons and rarely think about where my strengths, weaknesses, or quirky traits come from. Like precious family photo albums, they are locked in a trunk in the attic. Not lost. Just collecting dust.

3. I often am not connected with the daily lessons that are in front of me *today*. With a life overflowing—just like everyone else has—I focus, too often, on where I want to be as opposed to where I am now.

4. It is through living and sharing my life experiences that I keep my mom's legacy—as well as the legacies of my dad and brother—alive for my children. I am more than a son, a brother, or a dad. I am the connective tissue across generations.

5. I have an obligation to others to be a part of the lessons in their life. And I'm not just talking about with my children. I'm talking about anyone I have contact with. If I'm going to embrace the concept that life lessons can come from simple experiences, then I must be an eternal believer that I have the ability to impact others daily as well.

6. All of this is quite easy if you're not a bobblehead.

Why is any of this important? After all, it's just a bunch of old-fashioned common sense, right? What I can tell you is, for me, the simplistic quality of this has made it so easy to grasp and implement in my life. It's helped me slow down, be the dad I need to be, and pursue my dreams. It's validated the importance of what I do each day of my life. It's also helped me be content with the present—even when the present is plain old vanilla. Did having cancer play a part in this newfound outlook? Sure. But I hope you never have to confront a life-threatening illness to be able to grab hold of the potential power of this simple concept and apply it to your own life.

I loved that summer. As I will every summer yet to come. But I'm learning there is much to love about fall.

And winter.

And spring.

And as I move to the next season of my life, I'm going to make sure I love everything about what's most important.

The lessons I'm living today.

Lesson 25

Lessons

happen

every day.

Your Turn to Discover!

If you find yourself in a reflective mood after one or more chapters, I hope these questions help you rediscover some of your own life lessons. A more detailed list of questions—as well as a book club discussion outline—can be found on my website, www.BobbleheadDad.com.

CHAPTER 1: Some Things You Don't Want to Inherit
The scariest bogeyman is the one in your head.

- What did you fear as a child?

- How do you deal with your own fears?

- What's the biggest fear you need to overcome today?

CHAPTER 2: Why Painters Use Drop Cloths
Loved ones die, but they never leave.

- Who have you lost?

- What impact has the loss of a loved one had on you?

- How can you keep a lost loved one a part of your life today?

CHAPTER 3: Playing Post Office
Clean your desk. Clear the clutter. Then focus.

- How did your parents deal with stress?

- How do you deal with bigger issues in your own life?

- Is there an issue needing your attention today?

CHAPTER 4: I'm Sorry, What Did You Say?
Welcome good advice with action.

- What's the best advice you've ever received?
- Who have been the important teachers in your life?
- What advice do you need to follow today?

CHAPTER 5: Give and Take
The best caregivers have received the best care.

- As a child, were you more of a caregiver or a receiver?
- Who taught you how to care for others?
- Do you need more balance in being both a caregiver and receiver?

CHAPTER 6: I Can't Believe You Said That
When you can't be brilliant with words, be brilliant with your arms.

- Can you think of a time when—as a child—someone said exactly the right (or wrong!) thing to you?
- Are you a person who tries to fix a situation with words?
- Is there someone who needs a hug from you today?

CHAPTER 7: Mom and Dad Were Doing It
Meaningful tears fall from eyes that know how to laugh.

- Are your childhood memories filled with laughter?
- How do you deal with stress or pressure in your life?
- Is there a part of your life, today, that needs more laughter?

CHAPTER 8: Growing into My Running Shoes
There's only one person stopping you from being who YOU were meant to be.

- Were you labeled as anything specific as a child, such as unathletic, geeky, or awkward?
- When have you surprised yourself with your own abilities or talents?
- Do you have a label you need to shed today?

CHAPTER 9: Mum's the Word
Unless you have a gardener, you're in charge of splitting your own mums.

- Were you raised in a family of "joiners"?
- Do you have a hard time saying "no" to a request?
- Is there a part of your life—right now—that needs to be simplified?

CHAPTER 10: The Real Dirt
Plant yourself in good soil.

- How "fertile" was the soil from your childhood?
- Who—or what—has made the soil in your life more fertile?
- Is there some soil in your life in need of nourishment today?

CHAPTER 11: That's Why They Call It Work
Work isn't everything.

- How did your parents view work and rest?
- When did you last feel recharged?
- Do you need to schedule downtime or reprioritize things in your life?

CHAPTER 12: Summertime, and the Livin' Is Easy
Rest.

- Did your family play together when you were a child?
- Who do you enjoy relaxing with?
- Do you need to encourage people in your life to rest?

CHAPTER 13: Here Comes Santa Claus
The first step to achieving is believing.

- What did you believe in as a child?
- Where do you find strength when faced with adversity?
- What do you need to believe in today?

CHAPTER 14: Lifeguard on Duty
Lifeguards are always on duty.

- Were you raised in a family that helped others?
- Who are your lifeguards?
- Who do you need to help today?

CHAPTER 15: Will You Sign My Yearbook?
Say it. Write it. Today.

- As a child, who gave you encouragement and positive comments?
- When have you missed an opportunity to tell someone something important?
- Is there a message you need to share with someone today?

CHAPTER 16: Ob-la-di, Ob-la-da, Life Goes On
Life flies. Watch your time.

- As a child, who were the people in your life who seemed to live a rich, full, adventurous life?

- Do you dream about rediscovering yourself?

- Is it time to make a change in your life? If so, what's holding you back?

CHAPTER 17: I Wish They All Could Be California Girls
Ask. And you just might receive.

- Who was your most trusted friend as a child?

- When you are in need, who do you turn to?

- Is there someone you need to lean on for help today?

CHAPTER 18: Camp Songs
There's a camper—and a counselor—inside us all.

- Who cheered for you when you were a child?

- In what areas of your life do you need encouragement and support?

- Who needs to hear you cheer today?

CHAPTER 19: Whipped Cream Wonders
Celebrate something every day.

- What were your favorite celebrations as a child?

- Do you tend to celebrate or entertain?

- What do you need to celebrate today?

CHAPTER 20: I'd Rather Be the Jackson Five
Embrace who you are.

- What role did you play in your family as a child?
- Has your relationship with siblings and other family members changed over time?
- Are there things you can do to strengthen and improve relationships with your family?

CHAPTER 21: But I Want a Puppy!
The best gifts find you. Let it happen.

- What were some of the best gifts you received as a child?
- What is the most cherished gift you received as an adult?
- Is there something preventing you from receiving the gifts that are waiting for you today?

CHAPTER 22: I Hate You, Donny Osmond
Life is a series of transitions. Eventually, you need to move on.

- As a child, was it easy for you to move on to new things and experiences?
- When was the last significant "transition" in your own life?
- Is there something in your life today that is preventing you from moving forward?

CHAPTER 23: Dear Glady . . .
~~Don't strive for perfection.~~ *Be authentic. Be content.*

- Can you remember the feeling, as a child, of living a day when you felt totally alive and content?
- When is the last time you didn't want a day to end?
- What keeps you from living in the moment and embracing your days?

CHAPTER 24: Snoopin' in Mom's Purse
Expect the unexpected.

- Do you have a cherished keepsake from someone important to you?
- What are some of the simple moments from your past that have left a lasting impact on your life?
- Do you live for tomorrow at the expense of today?

CHAPTER 25: Wait, There's More!
Lessons happen every day.

- Do you feel connected to the lessons in your life?
- Do you contribute to the life lessons of others?
- Are you ready to start living today?

Congratulations. You are on your way to discovering your own life lessons. For additional reflective questions, please visit my website, www.BobbleheadDad.com.

IMERMAN ANGELS.org

1-on-1 cancer support

Connecting Cancer Fighters, Survivors & Caregivers

Dear Friend,

I hope *Bobblehead Dad* helps you discover the stories and lessons unfolding in your own life. Every day.

One of the most valuable lessons I received in my cancer journey was experiencing, firsthand, the power of one person helping another. It's the simplest act of humanity I have ever known.

Perhaps that's why I am so passionate about the organization with which I am gladly sharing proceeds from this book, Imerman Angels.

What I love most about Imerman Angels is their mission: they provide one-on-one cancer support to anyone, anywhere in the world. Free. They match up people who have been diagnosed with cancer with a survivor—of similar age, gender, and background—to provide support. And hope. They also match caregivers with other caregivers. All of the Imerman Angels mentors are people who can say, "I've been there. I beat this. And you can, too."

So, the next time someone you care about is told by his or her doctor, "I'm sorry. You have cancer," I hope you'll do two things:

1. Go back and read Chapter 6.

2. Tell them about Imerman Angels. Next to a huge hug from you, it just may be the best gift you give them.

Imerman Angels 1-on-1 Cancer Support
www.ImermanAngels.org
877-274-5529

Acknowledgments

It's tempting to say, as authors often do, thank you to "everyone who helped me in this journey." But then I wouldn't be following my own Lesson 15. I need to say it. I need to write it. Now.

First, to Sharon Boyd: You were the one person who gave me the initial encouragement to do this. You were the one who told me I could take a collection of stories for the kids and turn it into something bigger. You were the first person who said I could be a writer. Thank you for tirelessly cheering me forward. Thank you—and Julia Dupree—for your loving early edits. And thanks to your husband, Jim, for sharing you with me during this journey.

I truly had four great brothers growing up. To Kevin: keep laying the drop cloths, big brother. To Tom, Dave, and Mick—and my sisters-in-law Kathleen, Kathy, Lucy, and Carol—I send my love and thanks for always believing in me.

My life has been blessed with friends who have supported me through some dark hours. To Barry and Lori Reszel, Kevin Murphy, and Reverend John Hennessey, I reserve my deepest thanks. You were there for my family when I needed you the most.

To put it simply, my medical team, Dr. Richard Siebert and Dr. Tom Bormes, saved my life. Thank you. To Dr. Charles (Snuffy) Myers of the American Institute for Diseases of the Prostate: you are a brilliant and inspiring man and I am grateful for your ongoing guidance and care.

Thank you to Karen Jacobson and Chris Williams for giving me the two most treasured gifts ever. And thank you to Jon Appleget for words of wisdom that eventually sunk in.

This book took a few years to write. I'm not sure I would have continued to plug through edits after edits without my West Coast fan club: Pam Logan, Kathy Blauer, and Nancy May. And to Mark Clement, Daniel Russert, and Jennifer Polk, I extend my thanks for constantly telling me you believed in me. Your support came when I needed it most!

To my walking buddy and life guru, Jack Kraemer: you thought you were taking me on walks, didn't you? You actually launched me into the life I was meant to live.

To so many family members and friends, especially Arlis Higley, Jack Higley, Bev Harral, Mary Clauss, Sid and Patty Dillon, Helen and Duane Krause, and David and Denise Carr, I give my sincere appreciation.

Thank you to Reed Hoffmann for being my brother Kevin's extraordinary friend. Having your picture of Kevin in this book means the world to me.

To Jason Seiden, Jerry Zezima, Wade Rouse, Suzette Martinez Standring, Jenniffer Weigel, Jen Singer, Tracy Beckerman, Sandi Gehring, Annie Burnside, and Melinda Marchiano: I hope all of you know that your encouragement helped me believe in myself.

To my army of early readers, I send a huge shout out of thanks. Reading your reviews was honestly one of the best parts of this journey. I'm honored to be connected to each of you.

To my publisher, Greenleaf Book Group, my publicist, JKS Communications, and my amazing social media consultant, Rusty Shelton of Shelton Interactive, thank you all for helping make my dream come true.

To Jonny Imerman and the entire Imerman Angels family, I send love. You are changing the world and it is an honor to be one of you.

To the family of Heartsill Wilson, including Sandra Distel, Heather Schwarz, and Linda Dykstra: I cannot tell you how much your support and generosity have meant to me. It is an honor to help share your father and grandfather's beautiful words.

I find my greatest joy in life in my three children, Kevin, Wallis, and Drew. I'm proud to be your dad.

This book about fatherhood would never have been possible without being the son of a man who was truly the world's greatest dad. That would be my dad, Bob Higley. He taught me everything I know.

And lastly, to the two women I cherish most, my mom, Betty, and her best friend, Glady Dappen. While I'm sorry for sneaking so many peaks at the letters you wrote back and forth to each other, I hope you'll recognize a familiar writing style in my words. Glady, thank you for assuming the baton of motherly love from Mom when she left us way too early. And Mom, I hope this book just goes to show parents everywhere that, in a few short years, you truly can give your child a lifetime of lessons.

The Lessons Continue . . .

Like you, I love a good story. Maybe that's why I'm so excited to share with you something that literally happened in the few weeks before this book went to print.

The inspiring poem I found on the back side of that little piece of paper in my mom's purse actually never included an author's name. It was, in truth, simply a beautiful poem from an unknown voice—waiting patiently for me to rediscover it many years later.

As part of my research for this book, I learned that the man who originally penned that poem was named Heartsill Wilson. And while I was able to uncover a few facts about him, his life remained a mystery to me. I was even beginning to contemplate if I needed to remove his poem from the book because I didn't have proper permission to use it.

I suppose I should have paid closer attention to Lesson 24: Expect the unexpected.

Through the generosity of a Georgian artist named Darla Dixon, I was put in touch with Heartsill's granddaughter, Linda Dykstra.

Through Linda's all-embracing kindness, I was suddenly welcomed into the world of this man whose words had guided my own mother's life on a daily basis. I learned from Linda that the poem I found was written in 1954 and was originally titled "A Salesman's Prayer," but—because it quickly spread throughout the world, inspiring millions in over one hundred languages—it was appropriately re-titled "A New Day."

My deepest thanks go to Linda, her sister, Heather Schwarz, and their mother, Sandra Distel, for so graciously sharing so much with me about their father and grandfather. How spectacularly beautiful it is that a small piece of paper found by a young boy can—over thirty years later—bring two families and their mutual message of hope together.

Dr. W. Heartsill Wilson
1920-1994

Born in Marshall, Texas, Heartsill Wilson began his professional career as a used-car salesman after serving in World War II. His talents led him to Michigan where he moved through the ranks at Chrysler Corporation, ultimately becoming an executive with Plymouth.

Heartsill's true passion and calling, however, was motivational speaking, and he eventually left the automotive industry and spent the next thirty years of his life as a public speaker, a career that allowed him to touch, move, and inspire people around the globe.

It is an honor to share the story and message of Heartsill, a man whose life was grounded in his values, virtues, ethics, and integrity. His life embodied the belief that there is value to be discovered in every day!

To learn more about Heartsill, please visit my website at www.BobbleheadDad.com.

Join the conversation on Facebook!
Go to "Bobblehead Dad" and be sure to "*like*" it!
www.facebook.com/Bobblehead.Dad

You can also follow me on Twitter! @jimhigley